FAMILY WALKS
IN THE
WYE VALLEY

Heather & Jon Hurley

Maps by David Grech B.A., B.Arch., R.I.B.A.

Scarthin Books, Cromford, Derbyshire   1989

FAMILY WALKS
IN THE WYE VALLEY

Family Walks Series
General Editor: Norman Taylor

———————

THE COUNTRY CODE
Guard against all risk of fire
Fasten all gates
Keep dogs under proper control
Keep to paths across farm land
Avoid damaging fences, hedges and walls
Leave no litter
Safeguard water supplies
Protect wildlife, wild plants and trees
Go carefully along country roads
Respect the life of the countryside

———————

Published 1989.
Revised 1992.

Phototypesetting, printing by Higham Press Ltd., Shirland, Derbyshire

ISBN 0 907758 26 6

OLD TOLL HOUSE AT HOARWITHY

1

Dedication

To Alice, who arrived in time to share with us the joys of exploration and discovery.

―――――

The Authors

Heather Hurley has written several previous books about walking, including 'Wyedean Walks', and with her husband Jon, 'Paths and Pubs of the Wye Valley', 'Rambles and Refreshments on the Welsh Borders', and sixteen routes for the AA/OS Guide to the Wye Valley. As a voluntary warden, member of the Ramblers' Association and Chairman of the Ross Civic Society's Rights of Way Committee she has a wide experience of leading walks and knowledge of keeping footpaths open.

Jon Hurley has also had books published on poetry, wine, and pubs, and is currently working on novels. Like Heather he is a lover of the countryside and a keen gardener and golfer. With their three children they enjoy exploring the Wye Valley by foot, discovering its many hidden delights.

―――――

Acknowledgement

Thanks to Rosemary Jones for her help with typing.

CONTENTS

LOCATION OF WALKS

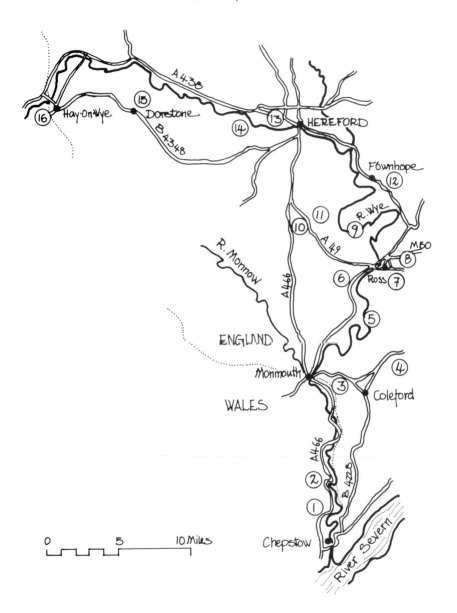

Introduction

The Wye Valley

The beautiful Wye Valley majestically follows the winding river, between high rocky outcrops, through flat flood plains and water meadows, constantly fed by a myriad of small clear streams. Walking terrain is ever changing, one minute steep, stony and breathtaking, then a relaxing stroll along a high ridge or through a steep sided valley in the sun. Children will be amused and enchanted, wandering through a countryside soaked in history; gaunt, once defensive castles, stand on windy hills, iron age forts abound, now alas overgrown and mere dots on the map, but always worth a climb to investigate. Churches and chapels of all descriptions, together with ivied and ruined monasteries appear waiting to be explored.

Birds, many unfamiliar, twitter secretly in hedgerows or brazenly wheel above on warm air currents. Badger, fox, deer, stoat and even otter may be observed if one is stealthy. Fields, lanes and woods are crowded with wild flowers, reds, pinks, yellows and blues, all bright in the midday sun or drooping in summer showers. Everywhere there are trees, fine English hardwoods, plantations of evergreens, flowering shrubs and many types of mosses and ferns covering banks and walls of ancient byways.

Family Walks

These sixteen original walks, all following public rights of way, in the Wye Valley, have been carefully chosen with the family in mind. Short strolls are interesting enough for the very young while more strenuous rambles provide a needed challenge to older children. Our baby daughter happily accompanied us on all these walks, first inside, then in a sling or carrier during the months it took to compile this book. When available her big brothers joined us to make the complete family picture.

While picnics in disused graveyards, in sunny sunken lanes, or sheltering from rain under dripping trees, have a certain charm, some walkers may prefer a pint in a pub nestling in some stonebuilt village. Perhaps a sticky bun, a bottle of pop and a packet of crisps from the village store may prove sufficient. Whatever, a refreshment break is essential and is an incentive to the reluctant younger participant.

Walkers are advised to carry the relevant Ordnance Survey sheets to be used in conjunction with the sketch maps shown in the book. When map reading use churches, buildings, woods and rivers as landmarks. Other items required are sensible footwear, lightweight waterproofs and a rucksack to carry refreshments, maps, compass, first aid and money.

The description of each walk is correct at the time of writing, but changes in the landscape do occur in rural areas, and some descriptions may vary according to the seasons. The pubs featured welcome children and walkers, but do remove those dirty boots before entering. There are very few public car parks in the Wye Valley, so when parking in villages or along roadsides, please do park safely and without obstructing field gates and farm entrances.

PATH FROM PORTHCASSEG

6

Symbols used on the route maps

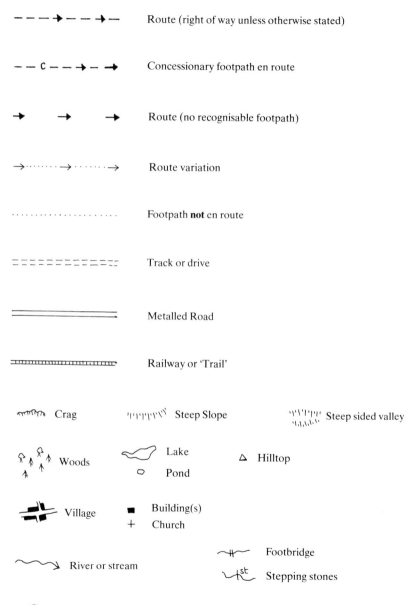

Route (right of way unless otherwise stated)

Concessionary footpath en route

Route (no recognisable footpath)

Route variation

Footpath **not** en route

Track or drive

Metalled Road

Railway or 'Trail'

Crag   Steep Slope   Steep sided valley

Woods   Lake   Hilltop
           Pond

Village   Building(s)
             Church

River or stream   Footbridge
                     Stepping stones

④ etc. Number corresponds with route description

365 STEPS

365 Steps: Wyndcliff

Outline   Lower Wyndcliff ~ Eagle's Nest ~ Porthcasseg ~ Upper Wyndcliff ~ Lower Wyndcliff

Summary   If walking in the footsteps of the poet William Wordsworth is unlikely to excite the energetic toddler, then the well worn slippery steps, all three hundred and sixty five of them leading to the Eagle's Nest, may do the trick. After a breathtaking climb to this panoramic viewpoint the walk flattens out with wide expansive views of the surrounding hills, farms and the Wye and Severn Valleys. Ancient gnarled yews, shallow caves and huge rocky boulders all add interest before returning through a quiet avenue of coppiced trees.

Attractions   The climbing of the 365 steps offers a challenging ascent to young and old alike. The steps were constructed in 1828 as a tourist attraction during the Romantic Period of the 18th and 19th centuries when it became fashionable for poets, writers and artists to visit this site of 'untamed beauty'. In 1971 the steps were renovated by army apprentices and are maintained by the Wye Valley Wardens. Twisting and turning, the 365 steps lead steeply up the cliff between moss covered boulders, past gaping caves, under ivy clad trees and across a rocky gully to reach the famous viewpoint at the Eagle's Nest.

The Eagle's Nest is a scenic lookout standing at 700 feet above the river Wye where a magnificent view of the Wye Valley will be enjoyed. A great horseshoe bend of the Wye encircles the Lancaut and a site known as Wintour's Leap can be seen on the sheer cliff opposite. During the Civil War a royalist, Sir John Wintour from the Forest of Dean, was chased by Parliamentarians and escaped by riding his horse down the sheer cliffs and across the Wye to safety in Monmouthshire (now Gwent). A more likely tale is that he dismounted his horse, climbed down the rocks and swam across the river.

Part of the walk is through ancient woodland where hazel, ash, oak, maple, spindle and yew have grown undisturbed for hundreds of years. The twisted roots and branches of the yews are well worth studying. One can easily imagine animal and serpent shapes in these, the oldest of all British trees. A small beech plantation provides an ideal place for children to run between the young upright trees.

The Wye Valley Walk is a waymarked path of fifty odd miles leading through beautiful countryside from the Welsh town of Chepstow to the

continued on page 12

9

Route 1

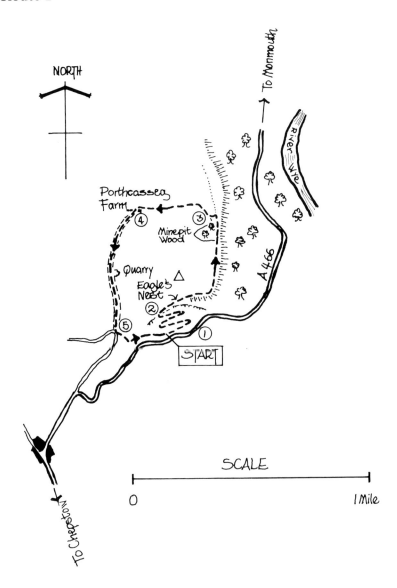

Route 1

365 Steps

3 miles

START   from the Lower Wyndcliff car park (OS Sheet 162 GR 527973) both sides of the A466.

ROUTE

1. *Keep right of the rocky face of a disused quarry, go past an information board and follow the sign to the start of the 365 steps. The stone and wooden steps zig-zag steeply up to the top of the Wyndcliff.*

2. *At the top of the cliff turn right along the waymarked route of the Wye Valley Walk to the Eagle's Nest viewpoint. Then continue along the path for a further half a mile through Minepit Wood, identified by its overgrown pit holes.*

3. *Leave Minepit Wood and the route of the Wye Valley Walk by bearing left over a gate leading into level fields. Turn left through an open gateway then sharp right along a hedge to Porthcasseg Farm.*

4. *At the farm turn left and follow a track passing an old quarry before reaching a tarmac lane.*

5. *Turn left at the lane and enter the Upper Wyndcliff picnic site. Follow the waymarked path down wooden steps and at the bottom bear left to return to the quarry car park.*

ACCESS BY BUS
    To Lower Wyndcliff from Chepstow and Monmouth.

GREEN WOODPECKER
green/red/black   32cm.

Cathedral City of Hereford. The yellow arrowed route will shortly be extended to Hay-on-Wye. It is under the care of the Wye Valley Countryside Service who provide leaflets, map packs and information boards.

Minepit Wood is a reminder of the days when iron ore was dug out and transported to iron furnaces at Tintern, An ancient pack horse road led from Porthcasseg (or Pony Way) to Tintern before the construction of the main road in the 1820s. From Porthcasseg Farm a gentle descent through fields and woodland leads back to the Lower Wyndcliff.

Refreshments Bring your own packed lunch or tea and make use of the scenic picnic site at Lower Wyndcliff.

TINTERN ABBEY

12

Penterry Church: Tintern and Penterry

Outline   Tintern Abbey ~ Penterry Church ~ Glyn Wood ~ Tintern Abbey

Summary   This strenuous but superb walk starts and ends on ancient cobbled cart tracks, leading to and from Tintern with its beautiful ruined abbey overlooking the river Wye. Between are hazel-canopied lanes, winding roads, woodland tracks, hilly fields dotted with snoozing sheep, and dried up water courses. It is a walk that makes one feel invigorated and should not unduly tax the sturdy child who will always be engrossed looking out for quite a number of interesting historical features. Classic Lower Wye Valley views are everywhere, glimpses of white cottages perched on hillsides, the gleaming river below sliced into silvery sections by slender firs, leaf strewn woodland floors dusted with late sunshine and the bark and call of unfamiliar wildlife.

From an uphill start along the Wye Valley Walk, little used paths lead to an isolated church at Penterry. From here the way descends to Glyn Woods and Chapel Hill back to Tintern, where ample parking, cafes, pubs, souvenir and craft shops offer a variety of goods and services which appeal to all members of the family.

Attractions   Tintern Abbey is renowned for its picturesque setting on the banks of the river Wye and the roofless ruins of the 12th century Cistercian Abbey are open to the public all the year round. Until 1756 the interior of the building was full of tumbling masonry and overgrown with saplings, but a forward thinking Chepstow man employed a hundred workmen to clear the site. It is now maintained by Welsh Heritage and a guide to its history is available at the Abbey's entrance.

Supervised by the monks, iron workings were established at Tintern and it became an important industrial centre in the 17th century for wire works, iron furnaces and forges. Many of the cobbled and paved tracks seen here were probably pack horse roads, widened to take wheeled traffic, which carried raw materials for the ironworks. Today they are shaded by overhanging trees and deep rooted green ferns growing lushly between mossy rocks. The smell of damp vegetation, while not unpleasant, stirs memories of travellers from the past coping with the narrow, hilly and uneven byways.

On the hillside surrounded by fields stands the remote and tiny church at Penterry. Enclosed by an ancient stone wall and partly

continued on page 16

Route 2

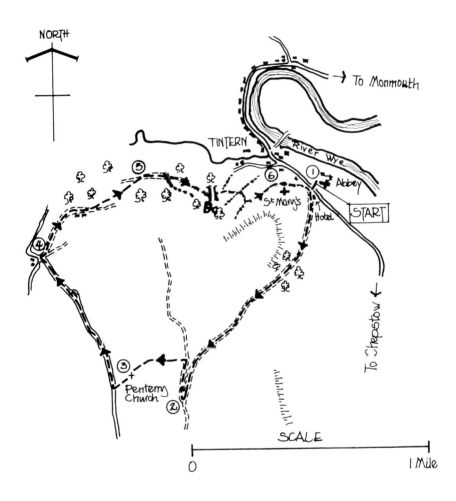

Route 2

Penterry Church   4½ miles

START   *at the Abbey car park (OS Sheet 162 GR 533001) at Tintern.*
ROUTE

1. *From the Abbey car park cross over the main road, turn right along a tarmac lane signed "Wye Valley Walk". Keep left at a 'T' junction where the lane becomes a rocky track behind hotel buildings. Ascend through woodland, then leave the waymarked route, continuing ahead till reaching another tarmac lane.*

2. *Follow this to the right for 300 yards, but before it bears left, turn left through a gateway into a field. Keep the hedge on the right and enter the next field by a gate. The right of way bears diagonally left to Penterry church concealed behind some tall trees.*

3. *Leave the churchyard by the opposite gate and follow a path going right to a gate in the corner of the field. Turn right along a narrow tarmac lane and follow this down to a crossroads.*

4. *Here turn right, following a bridleway, then take the left hand fork and proceed past two isolated cottages. At a sign to Bantam Cottage bear left and follow a waymarked woodland path down through Glyn Woods which leads eventually to a forest track.*

5. *Turn right along this track past a scenic viewpoint with a picnic table. Shortly after veer left along an enclosed path, and at a sign to Box Cottage be sure to keep ahead along a narrow path which steeply descends turning left under a makeshift wooden bridge. Take the next path to the right over a brook and at a junction with a sign 'Forest Trail' bear left to reach the ruined remains of St. Mary's church.*

6. *Continue past the church along a path which winds down to join a road. Follow this to the right and retrace your steps to Tintern Abbey.*

ACCESS BY BUS
    To Tintern from Chepstow and Monmouth.

concealed by a huge yew, the stone building boasts a bell turret with the addition of an ugly yellow brick porch. Local tradition suggests a village here was destroyed by the Black Death known to have ravaged the area in 1349.

A pretty lane winds down through scenic countryside to Glyn Woods where tall beech and oak trees cover the steep sided valley. Small clusters of holly offer protection to saplings from browsing animals. The narrow path is covered with centuries of dried leaves which pleasantly rustle underfoot.

In Glyn and Chapel Hill Woods the Forestry Commission has laid out picnic sites, viewpoints and forest trails. Leaflets on these are available from the Tourist Information Centre at Tintern.

At Chapel Hill there is another interesting site to explore, the ruined remains of St. Mary's, built in 1886 on the site of an earlier church probably founded by the monks. This building was apparently burnt down some years ago and at present there are no signs of restoration. After investigating the nooks and crannies of this ruin walk through the graveyard, overgrown with a variety of wild flowers, and enjoy a fine view of the abbey at Tintern and of the Wye Valley below.

Refreshments   Hotels and tea rooms at Tintern.

THE ROUND HOUSE

Naval Temple: The Kymin and Wyesham

Outline   Kymin ~ Wyesham Lane ~ May Hill ~ Kymin

Summary   Though short, this is a strenuous walk offering a stiffish challenge to all the family. It has, however, the advantage of a wayside inn half way round to enable everyone to tackle the steep slope back to the start in good heart. Views from the Kymin at 800 feet are panoramic with wide sweeps of Monmouth town set against a magnificent range of blue misted hills. The route follows two waymarked sections of the Offa's Dyke path, crosses green fields and along deep stone-walled lanes where great boulders and gnarled yews make interesting features to climb upon and explore. Wild flowers and bracken-clad hills, serried thickets and majestic hardwoods wait to be identified. Returning to the pinnacle of the Kymin a rest is enjoyed before viewing the Naval Temple, Round House and the glorious wrap-around scenery.

Attractions   The Naval Temple, Round House and viewpoint at the Kymin provide important and interesting features on this fairly demanding walk. The Temple, which at the time of writing is being restored, commemorates sixteen admirals of the late 18th century. Nelson, Hood and Hawke are familiar but have you heard of Duncan, Warren, Gell and others named on the medallions? This unusual monument was opened in 1801 and a year later was visited by Admiral Lord Nelson when he was touring the Wye Valley. More information about Nelson and his connection with this area can be obtained from the Nelson Museum in Monmouth.

The Round House with its surrounding landscaped grounds was constructed in 1793 to enable the wealthy young bucks of Monmouth to meet and disport themselves at this delightful, private and inaccessible site. Meals were taken in an upper banqueting hall, views enjoyed from a powerful telescope which stood on a flat roof, and games were played on the bowling green. This magnificently scenic site is now under the care of the National Trust who have owned the property since the early 1900's. Now everyone can admire the extensive views of the Wye Valley, Black Mountains and the Forest of Dean.

From the Kymin a short stretch of Offa's Dyke Path is followed. This is part of a scenic waymarked route of 168 miles along the Welsh Borders, leading from Prestatyn in North Wales to Chepstow in the south. Sections of the path follow the line of an historic 8th century dyke constructed by King Offa, ruler of Mercia.

continued on page 20

Route 3

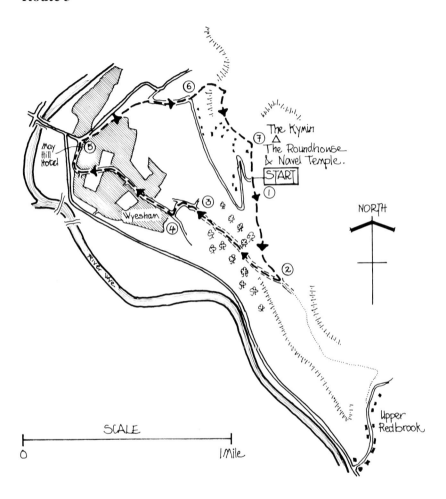

Route 3

Naval Temple 3½ miles

START   *from the National Trust car park at the Kymin (OS Sheet 162 GR 528126) reached by a signed road leading off the A4136 near Monmouth.*

ROUTE

1. *At the Kymin car park follow Offa's Dyke path signed to 'Upper Redbrook' along a narrow path leading into open fields. Keep to the right hand hedges till reaching a green lane and Cockshoot Ash Barn.*

2. *Leave the waymarked route and turn sharp right following the gently descending green lane into Wyesham.*

3. *At a fork bear left and pass a white-washed cottage called Greenbanks, then continue along the lane which veers left before meeting a road.*

4. *Turn right along the road through Wyesham.*

5. *At the May Hill Hotel turn right to re-join the waymarked route of Offa's Dyke Path which proceeds along the main road for a few yards before following a path signed to 'The Kymin and Naval Temple'. It steeply ascends above the road, through trees, across a meadow and along a short stretch of tarmac lane.*

6. *Continue ahead as indicated and follow the steep winding path through Garth Woods, across open hillside and into Beaulieu Woods where uneven stone steps lead up to the Kymin.*

7. *Turn right and pass the Round House, the viewpoint and the Naval Temple before returning to the car park.*

ACCESS BY BUS

   To Monmouth from Ross-on-Wye, Hereford and Coleford.

OX-EYE DAISY

white/yellow centre
May-September

Wyesham Lane is a fine example of an ancient byway, sunken from years of use, lined with leaning moss covered stone walls, shaded by beech hedges and old yews struggling out of rocky crevices. Nature has taken over the wayside quarries where willow herb and purple foxgloves sprout amongst tall ferns.

Wyesham, a busy suburb of Monmouth, has its own church, school and shops tucked in below the wooded slopes of the Kymin. The market town of Monmouth can be easily reached by crossing the Wye Bridge. Our route, however, keeps to the east bank of the Wye and continues up steep woodland paths, eventually returning breathlessly to the Kymin.

Refreshments   May Hill Hotel, Wyesham.

CANNOP PONDS

Forest Ponds: Cannop Ponds

Outline   Lower Pond ~ Folder's Green ~ Upper Pond ~ Lower Pond.

Summary   Sauntering through the Forest of Dean with its canopy of English hardwoods above a carpet of bluebells, wood anemones and celandines, provides a wonderful and perfectly safe ramble for parents, and children of all ages. This scenic and undemanding stroll tours the boundary of the placid, sky-reflecting Cannop Ponds, a man made series of pools created to drive machinery in earlier times, but now a haven for wild fowl, fish and water plants. There are rickety fallen tree 'bridges', marshy streams, gushing sluices and disused railway tracks to discover in this delightfully natural, sensibly-managed wood.

Attractions   The outstanding feature of this walk are the Cannop Ponds, attractively sited in the midst of the Forest of Dean. The Upper and Lower Ponds were created by damming the Cannop Brook at the beginning of the 19th century to provide water power for the iron works at Parkend. The pools remain as a tranquil reminder of earlier days when iron and coal were extensively mined in the Forest of Dean and transported by a network of railroads and tramways. During this century a gradual change has taken place transferring the once industrialised forest to a scenic and recreational one managed by the Forestry Commission.

At the start of the walk small streams are encountered flowing from hidden springs. This forms a marshy area where it is fun to cross the boggy places by balancing along fallen, lichen covered branches in a magical oaken grove. The waters of the Cannop Brook are regulated by a series of weirs and sluices both on its approach, and, after flowing through the ponds. Clear shallow streams strewn with moss-covered rocks make ideal paddling pools on a hot summer's day under the shade of the old Dean Forest oaks.

At Folder's Green the Forestry Commission have created a pleasant picnic site with parking, information board, tables and seats overlooking the Upper and Lower Ponds which are divided by a bridge and weir. The disused railway track was originally a tram road called the Severn and Wye. It was relaid as a railway line in 1868 and continued in use until 1963.

This short stroll is so full of interest, it is impossible to identify everything. At the water's edge moss, ferns and reeds provide a sheltered

continued on page 24

21

Route 4

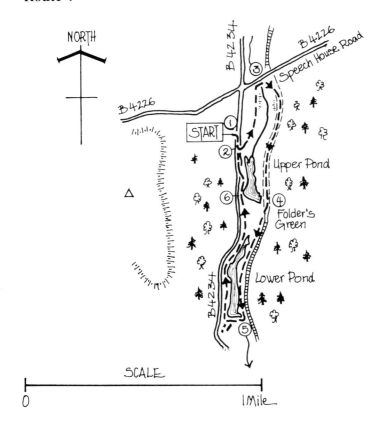

Route 4

Forest Ponds

2½ miles

START *from Forestry Commission parking (OS Sheet 162 GR 607113) on the B4234 at Cannop crossroads.*

ROUTE

1. *From the car park cross the B4234, turn right along the road for 50 yards until reaching a narrow path on the left beside a black and white road marker.*

2. *Follow this path, bearing left around the marshy extremities of the Upper Pond, and along the banks of the Cannop Brook. Climb a steep slope to join a grass covered path alongside the Speech House Road.*

3. *Turn right following the grassy path across a culverted brook on to a disused railway track which leads to the opposite side of the pond.*

4. *At Folder's Green with its excellent picnic site keep ahead along the wide track or, alternatively, take the more attractive path along the banks of the Lower Pond.*

5. *Turn right across a footbridge re-crossing the Cannop Brook. Pass the stone works and bear right to follow an uneven path which continues around the Lower Pond.*

6. *Upon reaching the Upper Pond, keep ahead till the winding path joins the road. Turn right back to the car park.*

ACCESS BY BUS

To Mireystock, Upper Lydbrook (2 miles from Cannop), from Coleford or Ross-on-Wye.

STITCHWORT

white   May-August

23

habitat for ducks, moorhens and coots. In spring, stitchwort, celandine, wood sorrel and bluebells make a delightful picture in this mixed woodland. Buzzards, finches, wrens and tits fly above pools now well stocked by Angling Clubs with tench, bream, perch and chub.

Towards the end of this walk the hectic cutting, loading and transporting of stone can be heard and seen at the last surviving stone works in the Forest of Dean. The Pennant stone quarried nearby is now only used for monumental and ornamental work.

This route is one of many that can be followed around Cannop Ponds. Walkers will notice the familiar Rambler's Association's yellow arrows marking their waymarked path and the red arrows of a Forest Walk laid out by the Forestry Commission. Leaflets describing these can be obtained from Tourist Information Centres at Ross or Coleford.

Refreshments Take your own and make use of a wide range of superb picnic sites.

THE WYE AT SYMOND'S YAT

Route 5
4 miles

Yat Ferry: Symond's Yat East and West

Outline   Symond's Yat East ~ The Biblins ~ Symond's Yat West ~ Symond's Yat East.

Summary   This is an exciting walk for both adults and children. It starts with a level stretch along the disused track of the old Ross to Monmouth railway which runs alongside the banks of the broad, and, at this particular point, rapid river Wye. It is a walk for the curious; lots of little nooks and crannies into which young heads may poke. There is a swaying suspension bridge across the river, dripping wells, caves, mines, lime kilns, inviting rocks to climb —all ending with the delightful ferry trip. Yat East and West has an air of the seaside, with bright cafes and hotels, quaint riverside pubs, boats and tourists buying scenic postcards of this lovely wooded gorge. Half way along there is even a little shop where children may be allowed to purchase ices and sweets while their parents sip a welcome cup of tea. An easy level walk suitable for pushchairs, expectant mothers and grandparents. The ferry crosses the Wye at all times except during heavy floods. If in doubt ring Symonds Yat (0600) 890232.

Attractions   Symond's Yat is a scenic riverside village divided by the river Wye which dramatically flows through this delightful wooded and rocky gorge. It is a busy popular place for tourists and locals alike, renowned for its famous view of the horseshoe bend from the 500 foot high Yat Rock. The view point can be reached by road or footpath from Symonds Yat East.

The beginning of the walk follows the disused track of the Ross to Monmouth Railway which ran from 1873 till Beeching's closure in 1965. Several railway features remain, including old stations, blocked tunnels, dismantled viaducts and G.W.R. boundary markers. Stretches of this railway track now serve as part of the Wye Valley Walk, a recreational footpath leading from Chepstow to Hereford.

The unpolluted river Wye is a constant and lively feature on this walk. Glimpses of the beautiful river will be seen between the thick rows of alders and willows which line the bank. At the Rapids fast white water provides a difficult challenge for young canoeists who may occasionally be observed capsizing. Lone fishermen will also be spied either standing patiently on the bank or sitting sedately in a boat hoping to catch one of the Wye's salmon.

continued on page 28

25

Route 5

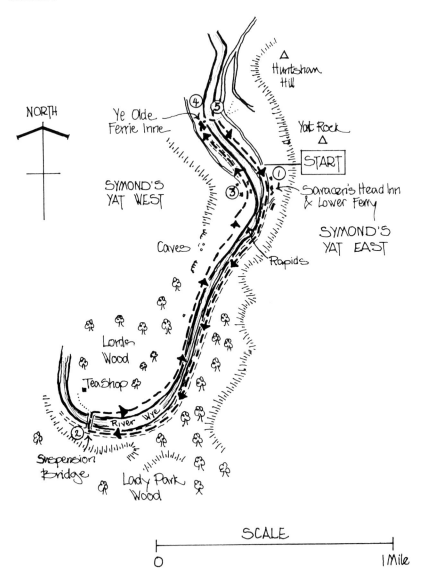

Route 5

Yat Ferry
4 miles

START *from Symond's Yat 'Pay and Display' riverside car park (OS Sheet 162 GR 561160).*

ROUTE

1. *Leave the car park and turn left past the Saracen's Head Inn and the lower ferry. The end of the tarmac lane leads on to the route of the disused railway track, now forming part of the waymarked Wye Valley Walk. Follow this alongside the riverbank for one and a half miles.*

2. *At the Biblins turn sharp right and cross the Wye by the suspension bridge. At the other side turn right and follow the riverside path for a further mile and a half until you reach hotels and cottages at Symond's Yat West.*

3. *Upon meeting a tarmac lane, bear right along a track descending to the river and shortly a sign displays 'Unsuitable for Motor Vehicles'. Stay on this track, ignore the lower ferry, until you reach Ye Olde Ferrie Inne*

4. *Turn right and descend a steep flight of narrow stone steps leading through the inn to the landing stage. Hail the ferryman from inside the inn. He will take you across the river on payment of 40 pence for adults and 20 pence for children. (1988 prices)*

5. *On landing, turn right immediately and follow a field path along the riverside back to the car park.*

ACCESS BY BUS

To Whitchurch (one mile away) from Monmouth and Ross-on-Wye.

HAZEL CATKINS

early Spring

Off the beaten track lies an area called the Biblins, where in recent years a Childrens Adventure Centre, a bridge and a nature reserve have been established. The National Nature Reserve in Lady Park Wood is owned by the Forestry Commission. The major part of the reserve is left unmanaged and a footpath leads around the perimeter. The suspension bridge is a high, narrow structure built by the Forestry Commission in 1957. Only six persons at a time may cross and they are warned not to bounce or sway the bridge. A sign on the opposite bank indicates the way to a remotely sited tea shop.

Steep, overgrown cliffs are more obvious on the west side of the Wye. The sound of running water leads one to investigate the Dropping Wells, an interesting formation of limestone rocks and caves where water drips over disused iron ore mines. From here to Yat West the craggy cliffs are dotted with caves, mines and old quarries. Care should be taken if these old workings are to be explored, and children need to be accompanied by an experienced adult with a powerful torch. From the 17th century till 1820 iron ore was carried from the mines to the New Weir Forge. The outline of this extensive iron works can still be seen under many years of undergrowth.

The Symond's Yat ferries are a pleasant reminder of bygone days. The lower ferry operated by the Saracen's Head Inn formed part of an ancient route, and the upper crossing at Ye Olde Ferrie Inne was used extensively during the early 1900's. Before this a larger boat was also kept to convey livestock and goods across the river. Both ferries operate all year round except during floods.

Refreshments   There is no shortage on this walk:- Saracen's Head Inn, Yat East, with terraced beer garden overlooking river Wye. Biblins Tea Shop. Ye Olde Ferrie Inne, Yat West, with extensive terraced beer garden beside the banks of the Wye. Hotels and tea rooms.

Luke Brook: Glewstone

Outline   Glewstone ~ Daffaluke ~ Glewstone

Summary   This is a delightful walk in a quiet corner of Herefordshire where a rural landscape of fields and orchards can be viewed from the banks of the Luke Brook and from winding country lanes. An evening in early May is the best time to appreciate the acres of apple blossom, cheerful bird song and an abundance of wild flowers on this undulating ramble. Glewstone is a small village where houses and white-washed cottages cluster around a minor crossroads within a few minutes walking distance from the serene Wye.

Attractions   Glewstone is a typical residential village but a century ago things were very different when its inhabitants enjoyed a shop, smithy and two beer houses. Also, at the end of Boat Lane beside the river Wye there was a timber yard and yet another inn described as 'Glewstone Boat Beer House and Garden'. Here a busy ferry carried passengers and goods across the Wye to Walford.

   The Luke Brook is a narrow stream where mallards swim between lush beds of watercress. The brook rises in the adjoining parish of Peterstow, and joins the Garron Brook before flowing into the Wye at Whitchurch. Its water once drove two waterwheel pumps and powered two watermills during the 19th and early 20th centuries.

   Surrounded by rows of apple trees, Glewstone is a marvellous sight at blossom time. The rich sandstone soil is ideal for fruit growing and the county of Herefordshire is also famous for its cider, made from particular types of small, sour apples. A Farm Shop along the route sells locally produced fruit and vegetables.

   Daffaluke is a tiny place with just one large house and a few farms. The name is derived from the Welsh dyffryn-llug, meaning 'valley of the marsh'. Two springs are shown on the map and these drain into the Luke Brook. The pretty lane leading back to Glewstone is lined with high banks of wild flowers. Children enjoy identifying bluebells, stitchwort, herb robert, cow parsley, celandines, and many more. Before returning they may also recognise the former village school, now sympathetically converted into a private dwelling.

   A last glimpse of the Luke Brook can be savoured from the 'Paper Mill Bridge'. *continued on page 32*

Route 6

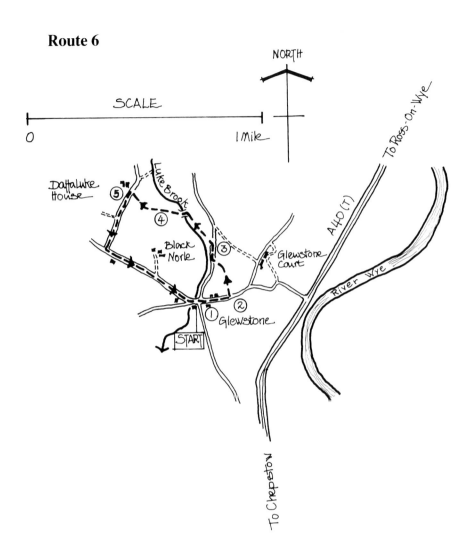

Route 6

Luke Brook

2 miles

START   *Half a mile from the A40 at Glewstone crossroads (OS Sheet 162 GR 559229). Park along roadside.*

ROUTE

1. *From the crossroads follow the road towards Ross for 300 yards. Beyond a row of white cottages turn left along a signed footpath.*

2. *Walk between fences over a stile, then ahead through orchards and across a stile on the left. Bear diagonally right across a paddock to a further stile at the right of a line of houses. Now turn right then left on to the road.*

3. *Keep to the right along the road for 100 yards, and beyond Yew Tree Cottage cross a stile on the left. Follow the undefined footpath along the right hand bank of the Luke Brook (or keep to the track on the left bank), then cross it by a narrow footbridge on the left. Bear right through orchards to a makeshift stile found in the right hand hedge.*

4. *Walk diagonally to the left across the meadow towards an oak tree, then keep to the left hand hedge to reach a gate leading on to a lane at Daffaluke.*

5. *Follow this to the left, and at the junction turn left to return to Glewstone.*

ACCESS BY BUS
    To Glewstone from Ross-on-Wye.

FOOTBRIDGE OVER LUKE BROOK

C

Refreshments Walkers are very welcome at Glewstone Court Hotel where tasty bar snacks may be eaten in their comfortable drawing room or attractive garden.

OLD TURNPIKE ROAD FROM DEEP DEAN

Route 7   3¼ miles
Chase Hill Fort: Coughton and Chase Hill

Outline Coughton ~ Hill Farm ~ Chase Hill ~ Coughton.

Summary A quietly winding lane forming a natural valley between wooded hills passes through a time warp to an abandoned route once used as a turnpike road that clattered to the sound of cart wheels and iron shod hooves. Now preserved as a public right of way it climbs and snakes through the fields and hills of Chase and Penyard. At Hill Farm the historic road continues meandering down to Ross-on-Wye, but our way turns left following the splendid waymarked Wye Valley Walk. This recreational path, clearly marked with yellow arrows wanders up to and around the steep ramparts of a hill fort used over 2,000 years ago by Iron Age men. From here the path steeply descends taking the walker through leafy woods and bright open fields before returning to Coughton.

Attractions The small hamlet of Coughton lies in the parish of Walford along the banks of the discreet Castle Brook, which flows through a picturesque valley surrounded by Penyard, Chase and Howle Hills. During the last century five corn, paper and tuck (wool) mills were driven by the waters of the brook. One of these sites is now used as a saw mill and another as a soft drink factory.

The route of an 18th century turnpike road is followed from Coughton to Hill Farm. It was one of eleven roads turnpiked by the Ross Trust in 1749, and in the Road Act of that year was described as 'the road leading from the said town of Ross, along Puckeridge Lane, to a Place called Dib Dean'. By 1791 the route was abandoned for being 'in many parts narrow and out of Repair', and was replaced by an easier road, still used today, through Coughton to Deep Dean. The renovated stone house beside the Castle Brook is said to have been an inn where 18th century travellers rested and took refreshments.

The Forestry Commission manages part of the woods covering the slopes of Penyard and Chase Hills. Plantations containing beech, chestnut, ash, spruce, birch and hazel grow above carpets of bracken and willow herb. Several common species of birds are heard in these woods, including wrens, pigeons, jays and magpie. It is especially rewarding in the autumn to gather hazel nuts, chestnuts and blackberries.

Before reaching Hill Farm a solitary oak recently provided some imaginative entertainment for groups of youngsters, who were prompted by a Countryside Warden to choose appropriate words to describe this

continued on page 36

33

Route 7

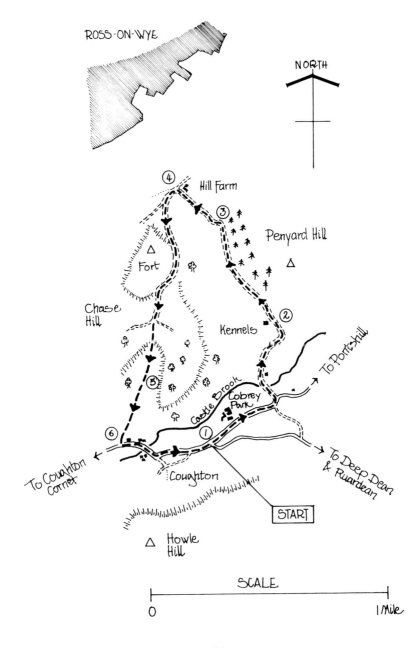

ROSS-ON-WYE

NORTH

④ Hill Farm

③ Penyard Hill

△ Fort

Chase Hill

Kennels

⑤

Castle Brook Cobrey Park

⑥

To Coughton Corner

Coughton

① START

To Ports Hill

②

To Deep Dean & Ruardean

△ Howle Hill

SCALE

0   1 Mile

Route 7

Chase Hill Fort

3¼ miles

START   At Coughton in Walford two miles south of Ross-on-Wye. Park on grass verge near junction of road to Ruardean and Deep Dean (OS Sheet 162 GR 606212).

ROUTE

1. From the road junction take the left hand fork along a road past Cobrey Park. Where the road bends left turn left along a sunken track signed 'Public Footpath'. Cross the bridge over Castle Brook and pass a renovated house before gently ascending to the wooded slopes of Penyard Hill.

2. On reaching modern buildings of the hunt kennels obstructing the right of way, bear right along a forestry track alongside the kennels. Where the track bears right cross a stile on the left to rejoin the right of way. Turn right after crossing the stile and walk along a deeply rutted and stony path leading to another stile,

3. Keep to the left hand hedge through a field passing a solitary oak on your left before reaching the next stile. Here turn right and follow the right hand fence until meeting a sunken lane leading past Hill Farm.

4. At Hill Farm turn sharply left and follow the yellow arrows of the Wye Valley Walk along a broad forest track which forks left after the barrier. This gradually ascends to the wooded ramparts of the Iron Age fort on the right. At an island of conifer trees bear left and continue ahead as indicated by the waymarks down a narrow steeply descending path.

5. At a field gate the Wye Valley Walk proceeds straight ahead downhill through fields towards farm buildings beside the road at Coughton.

6. Turn left along the road to return to the start.

ACCESS BY BUS

To Coughton Corner from Ross-on-Wye.

fine tree. The idea of looking at a given aspect of nature from various standpoints is an American one, it encourages country lovers to think afresh about natural features seen on walks.

The return from Hill Farm traverses more forestry land where scenic views are obtained before reaching the Iron Age hill fort standing at 600 feet. A single rampart encircles the cultivated interior of twenty two acres. There is no public access over the hill fort but the steep ramparts can be investigated by small children crawling through thick undergrowth to the summit. All ages will admire the earthworks for having survived a period of 2,000 years.

Children enjoy the steep slippery slope down Chase Hill strewn with small conglomerate rocks known as pudding stone. A number of narrow paths lead off the official Wye Valley Walk, which they may wish to explore.

Refreshments There are no inns or tea shops on this walk, so it is advisable to provide a picnic.

PLAGUE CROSS IN ROSS CHURCHYARD

Route 8   6½ miles

Rudhall Brook: Ross-on-Wye

Outline   Ross-on-Wye ~ Rudhall ~ Brampton Abbotts ~ Ross-on-Wye.

Summary   This is a more ambitious longer walk suitable for families with older children or those carrying babies in slings or carriers. Combined with a tour of the shops, buildings, stunning viewpoint and market of Ross-on-Wye this walk makes an interesting day trip which will appeal to teenagers. Starting from the town a level path leads through attractive water meadows beside the tranquil and shady banks of the Rudhall Brook. Quiet winding lanes are then followed from Rudhall to Brampton Abbotts where an ancient church makes a convenient break point. A less easy section then descends to the river Wye where the clearly waymarked Wye Valley Walk leads back to Ross-on-Wye.

Attractions   Ross-on-Wye is a busy market town nestling between the meandering river Wye and the wooded slopes of Chase and Penyard Hills. From as early as the 18th century Ross became a popular centre for tourists to explore the delights of the Wye Valley. A Ross Walkabout leaflet provides a guide to the town's sites of historical and architectural interest. It is available from book shops and the Tourist Information Centre.

The silent sullen waters of the Rudhall Brook are attractively lined with alders, willows, oaks and ash which provide quiet and shady cover for the odd mallard. Towards the end of summer a feast of elderberries, red currants, blackberries and hazel nuts can be plucked from the banks of the brook. The rarer spindle tree, whose horny wood is ideal for making spindles used for spinning wool by hand, is also found here. The tree is small, bearing bright red berries shaped like a priest's hat.

The mansion at Rudhall lies in a secluded hollow surrounded by tall trees and stone walls. The house dates from the 14th century with some later additions in various architectural styles. The Rudhall family lived here for several generations and their monuments can be inspected at Ross and Brampton Abbotts churches.

In summer the narrow lanes between Rudhall and Brampton Abbotts are bordered with purple mallow, red poppies, white campion, ox-eye daisies, blue scabious and garlands of sweet smelling honeysuckle.

Brampton Abbotts is a small village lying within one mile of Ross-on-Wye. Modern development has crept in between the scattered dwellings of earlier times. During the Norman period Brampton was

continued on page 40

37

Route 8

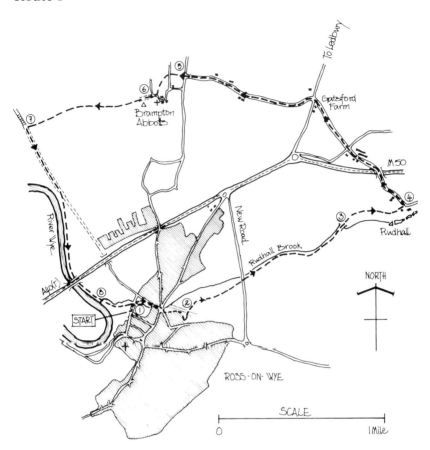

Route 8

Rudhall Brook

6½ miles

START *from the 'Pay and Display' car park in Edde Cross Street (OS Sheet 162 GR 598243) at Ross-on-Wye.*

ROUTE

1. *Turn left down Edde Cross Street and cross the bridge over the Rudhall Brook, then turn immediately right along a signed footpath leading to Greytree Road. Follow this to the right. At a road junction keep ahead into Millpond Street. Beside a car park turn left to follow a narrow path alongside the Small Brook. Cross the footbridge over the brook and keep left along a track to the disused railway track.*

2. *Proceed ahead through a gap in the embankment and follow the Country Landowners Association waymarks through a series of meadows to a new relief road not yet shown on OS maps. Walk up and over the road and follow a field path beside the Rudhall Brook till reaching a wide footbridge crossing the brook.*

3. *Here keep straight ahead to the right of a ditch shortly crossed by a bridge on the left. Bear diagonally right across the field to a farm track leading to the road at Rudhall.*

4. *Turn left along a quiet road which crosses over a motorway and keep ahead at a minor crossroads before reaching Gatsford Farm. Here cross the Ross/Ledbury road and follow a tarmac lane to a T-junction at Brampton Abbotts.*

5. *Walk straight ahead up a bank, over a stile and through a field to another stile leading on to a lane. Cross this and bear diagonally left through an orchard to a hidden stile found between two houses.*

6. *At Brampton Abbotts church keep right around the church and follow a signed path on the left leading between houses. At first it follows an enclosed track to a field where a stile ahead leads into a large arable field. The way is ill defined, but make a straight line through the crop or to avoid this, turn right and walk around the field to a stile in the right hand corner. Now bear left along a farm track leading to a disused railway line.*

7. *Turn left along the dismantled railway which now serves as part of the Wye Valley Walk. Yellow arrows indicate the way along the riverside and under the Ross Spur road to return to Ross-on-Wye.*

8. *Beyond the Boat House leave the Wye Valley Walk and bear left along a track to Edde Cross Street. Then turn right to the car park.*

owned by the Abbotts of Gloucester, but it was not till the Dissolution that the name Abbotts was added. A Norman nave and chancel can be seen in St. Michael's church together with a 14th century timbered porch and a small Rudhall memorial of 1507.

Near the end of the walk a disused track is followed. This was the route of the Hereford, Ross, Gloucester Railway which was opened on 1st June, 1855. Great festivities were held in Ross on that day to celebrate this great achievement. The station was gaily decorated and local children lined the platform to cheer the arrival of the first train. By the 1860s Great Western Railway took over the small company and at a later date it was absorbed by British Rail, who closed the line in 1964.

Refreshments Plenty of inns, cafes, restaurants to choose from in Ross-on-Wye.

ACCESS BY BUS
To Ross-on-Wye from Hereford, Gloucester, Ledbury, Monmouth and Forest of Dean.

THE WYE AT SELLACK

40

Route 9

Sellack Boat: Sellack

Outline   Kings Caple ~ Sellack Boat ~ Red Rail ~ Hoarwithy ~ Kings Caple.

Summary   This is a pleasant family walk in the Middle Wye Valley where picturesque countryside offers plenty of rural attractions, including a delightful stretch of the river Wye, three interesting churches and two bridges across the river. At Kings Caple there is ample parking and an inn at Hoarwithy is conveniently placed for refreshments half way round. Although Sellack Boat retains its name, the boat has long since been replaced by a suspension bridge making an exciting wobbly crossing of the Wye. Lush riverside meadows are grazed by a variety of animals and the surrounding fields are used for arable and soft fruit farming.

Attractions   Kings Caple lies on the eastern bank of the Wye within a large loop of the river. The church, dedicated to St. John the Baptist, stands in an elevated position offering splendid views from its graveyard. Its 14th century tower with a slender spire provides a prominent landmark throughout this ramble. The steep mound opposite is called Caple Tump and is the site of an early Norman castle, later used for fairs and festivities and now scheduled as an ancient monument.

Two other notable Herefordshire churches are seen on this walk; St. Tysillio at Sellack situated in a delightful sheltered spot near the banks of the river Wye and St. Catherine's at Hoarwithy. The latter is a unique Italian style edifice with a campanile tower and monastic cloisters overlooking the pretty riverside village of Hoarwithy. Designed by J. P. Seddon, a London architect, this oddly attractive church was built around an earlier chapel during the Victorian period.

Sellack Boat is soon reached, where a former ford and ferry were replaced in 1896 by the suspension bridge connecting Sellack and Kings Caple. The bridge crosses the river in one span of 190 feet, and from its swaying timber deck the timeless nature of the river may be savoured. At Red Rail 'ford of the street' is the site of a river crossing dating back to Roman times.

Before reaching Hoarwithy the route closely follows the banks of the river Wye, where evidence of fishing is clearly visible. Do not disturb the fishermen and keep at a distance to observe their skills. During the last century Hoarwithy was known for its salmon fishing and many of its inhabitants made a living from this precarious occupation. A steep short

continued on page 44

41

Route 9

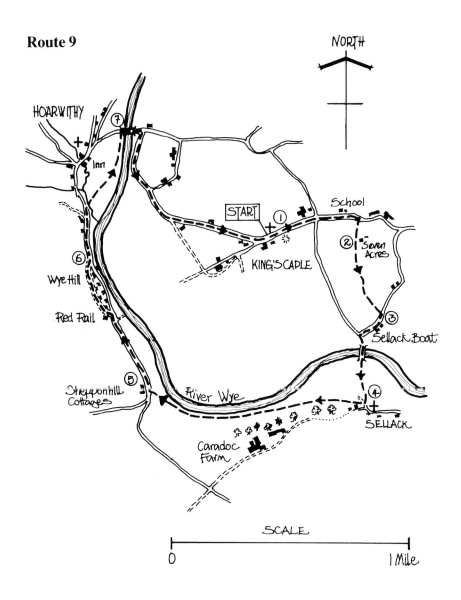

Route 9
Sellack Boat

START *from Kings Caple church (OS Sheet 149 GR 5⁵*
yards west of the crossroads.

ROUTE

1. *Facing Kings Caple church turn right along a tarmac lane and continue
   ahead at the crossroads. Pass the village school then turn right alongside
   a tall stone cottage following a track past a drive leading to a house
   called Seven Acres. At the end of the track cross a stile beside a field
   gate.*
2. *Walk in a straightish line through the fields, keeping to the hedge on the
   left to a stile. Cross this and continue in the same direction now with the
   same hedge on the right. Follow the hedge to its end and then cross an
   arable field to a gate and sign at a road.*
3. *Turn right along the road, past two cottages at Sellack Boat and bear left
   along a footpath to the suspension bridge. Cross the Wye and keep
   ahead along a well used field path leading to Sellack Church.*
4. *Beside the church cross a gate on the right where the right-of-way goes
   across a long meadow to meet the river bank at a stile. Now follow the
   banks of the Wye until reaching white-washed cottages at Shepponhill.
   Leave the riverside to bear diagonally left towards the cottages to reach
   the road by a gate.*
5. *Follow the road to the right for a quarter of a mile and upon reaching
   dwellings at Red Rail bear left up a signed path beyond Red Rail House.
   A well defined path climbs the bank leading to cottages at Wye Hill and
   then to Yew Tree Cottage where a sudden descent returns to the road.*
6. *A further short stretch of road is followed to the left before following a
   signed field path on the right leading diagonally right through meadows
   and over stiles to join the riverbank and bridge at Hoarwithy. (For the
   inn turn left at the bridge and follow the road into the village).*
7. *Cross the iron bridge and at the other side turn right along a wide track
   leading on to a tarmac lane which leads back to the church at Kings
   Caple.*

ACCESS BY BUS
   To Hoarwithy from Ross-on-Wye and Hereford.

to Wye Hill is well rewarded by excellent views of the river, ¬rwithy bridge and Kings Caple church.

Pretty stone and white-washed houses and cottages are attractively placed along the steep wooded bank at Hoarwithy. Apart from its church and inn, the village's other important feature is the distinctive and useful iron bridge. The original timber toll bridge was constructed in 1856 after the passing of the Hoarwithy Bridge Act. However, this was replaced 20 years later by the present iron structure. A well used horse ferry formerly operated between Hoarwithy and Kings Caple which carried foot passengers, goods and livestock across the river. The tall toll-house became redundant in 1935 when the bridge was de-tolled by the County Council. It is now a fishing lodge.

The winding lanes and field paths leading from Hoarwithy to Kings Caple pass fields full of cattle, racehorses, Welsh cobs and sheep, quietly grazing the rich pastures. Other land produces acres of crispy apples and juicy strawberries which can be self-picked when in season.

Refreshments   At the attractively situated New Harp Inn at Hoarwithy. Bar snacks and a lawned garden.

RUINED CHURCH AT LLANWARNE

44

Route 10 — 2 miles

A Ruined Church: Llanwarne

Outline   Llanwarne church ~ Donathan ~ Llanwarne Church.

Summary   This gentle two-mile amble starts from the Victorian church at Llanwarne, leads across arable fields, continues alongside a chattering brook through the outskirts of the village. It is an ideal walk for children and senior citizens. The first interesting site encountered is a small English vineyard followed by an easy climb to enjoy superb undulating views of distant hills with the occasional house or cottage perched halfway up protected by a windbreak of evergreens. The pretty Gamber brook constantly met en route, offers a pleasant diversion with its crystal clear water, varied bridges and flowering banks. The way back through the village is mainly on tarmac lanes, but a short footpath traverses a field skirting another tiny windswept vineyard before reaching the ghostly ruins of Llanwarne's former 13th century church.

Attractions   The Victorian church at Llanwarne was built in 1864 and dedicated as Christ Church. It stands in an elevated position next to a former school, now used as the village hall. Opposite this 19th century scene flows the Gamber Brook which rises in the adjoining parish of Much Birch and winds its way through fertile fields to join the Garron before entering the Wye at Whitchurch. See how many small fish and water plants can be spotted from the first bridge!

The vineyard was planted in 1985, and it will be another two years before grapes will be harvested to produce palatable wine. Meanwhile the owner is growing strawberries between the rows of vines. Guess the original purpose of the large house on the right? Yes — the rectory.

At the overgrown quarry layers of red sandstone are exposed. Feel the stone, it is very crumbly, and although it has been used for centuries as local building material, it does not weather well. Through the fields various birds will be noticed, including hovering buzzards occasionally escorted by a garrulous flock of crows. Numerous pigeons, a pest to the farmer, are seen grazing, roosting or speeding from one meal to another, and friendly robins may be enticed to share a few picnic crumbs.

Beside Donathan farm there is an idyllic spot, where an ancient stone slab stile leads on to a quiet lane. A narrow stone footbridge crosses the Gamber, but the ford has been replaced by a modern tarmaced culvert. It is not hard to imagine the slow turning, creaking wheels of Deacon's Mill which stood near this site till the mid 19th century.

continued on page 48

45

Route 10

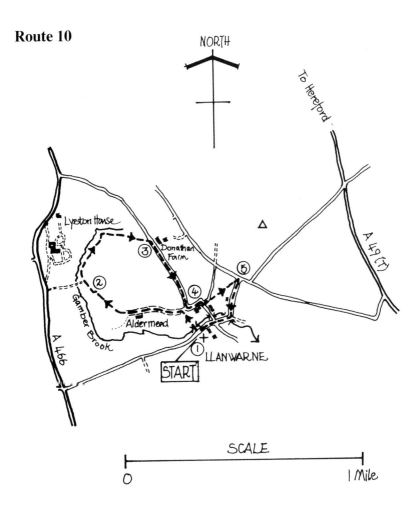

NORTH

To Hereford

A 49 (T)

Lyston House

Donathan Farm

③

②

④

⑤

△

Gamber Brook

Aldermead

A 466

① LLANWARNE

START

SCALE

0   1 Mile

Route 10

A Ruined Church

2 miles

START *opposite Christ Church at Llanwarne (OS Sheet 149 GR 505281).*

ROUTE

1. *Opposite the church follow the signed footpath leading straight ahead over a footbridge across the Gamber Brook, and continue through a vineyard to a stile in the right hand corner. Turn left along a tarmac lane for a few yards. This leads on to a farm track signed 'Aldermead'. Keep right of this property and follow the right fork alongside the left hand hedge of an arable field.*

2. *Turn left over a stile at the top of the incline where the right-of-way continues to the right on the other side of the hedge. Cross a stile in the right hand corner of this sloping field then follow the banks of the Gamber below on the left. Both brook and footpath bear right before passing a cottage called 'Little Field'.*

3. *Opposite Donathan Farm leave the field by a stone slab stile on your left. This leads on to a tarmac lane which is then followed to the right.*

4. *At a minor T-junction turn left and take the next left turn for approximately 30 yards, then follow a signed footpath on the right, going diagonally across a field to a stile leading into a tiny strip of a vineyard. Proceed in the same direction to a gap in the hedge leading on to the road.*

5. *Turn right along this road. Descend through the village to cross the Gamber for the last time before reaching the ruined church. A short walk ahead leads back to the start.*

ACCESS BY BUS

A one mile walk from the Hereford to Gloucester bus service which stops on the A49.

The walk through Llanwarne village provides plenty of interest, high stone walls, old houses, modern bungalows, and the now familiar trickling sound of Gamber Brook. From a rustic seat beside the war memorial the main feature on this walk, the picturesque ruins of Llanwarne's Norman church may be enjoyed. Enter the churchyard by the fine 15th century lych gate and view the medieval bell tower before exploring the nave and aisle still surrounded by surviving thick stone walls. Built adjacent to the annually flooding Gamber the church was abandoned in 1864 and replaced by the present church. If visited during the spring or summer a surprising number of wild flowers can be seen growing within the ruined walls.

Refreshments Bring your own drinks and snacks.

HIGGIN'S WELL

Higgin's Well: Little Birch

Outline   Little Birch Methodist Chapel ~ Higgin's Well ~ Lower Wriggle Brook ~ Little Birch Methodist Chapel.

Summary   Beginning at a 19th century Methodist Chapel at Little Birch, this varied and undulating route follows a green lane enclosed by thick hedges, which in autumn are garlanded with the bright fruit of hips, haws, guelder rose and snowberries, all festooned with old man's beard. A feature of this walk is the legendary Higgin's Well, a typical example of Victorian craftsmanship. Little Birch church provides a pleasant half way stop for a short rest, with inviting seats both in the churchyard and the sheltered porch. From here field paths descend steeply to cross the aptly named Wriggle Brook via a rustic bridge set in a delightful leafy dell. Quiet lanes and tracks then lead through the scattered village of Little Birch where children and adults will enjoy a variety of sheep, fowl, cattle, goats, donkeys, ponies and horses kept in small 'good life' orchards and paddocks.

Attractions   In Herefordshire during the 19th century the non-conformist movement was so popular that a vast number of different chapels were established, including the one at Little Birch, built as a Primitive Methodist Chapel in 1834. The present neat stone structure dates from 1858 and weekly Sunday services are still held. The width of the green lane opposite indicates an ancient route used for driving carts and stock. Its hedges contain a rich variety of trees, shrubs and flowers — see how many you can identify.

Higgin's Well is a 'lip' well with two levels, one for domestic use and the other for animals. A plaque inserted into the surrounding stone wall states that the well was 'restored and enlarged by public subscription to commemorate the Diamond Jubilee of Queen Victoria, 1897'. Higgin's Well enjoys a richly documented reputation in the neighbourhood as 'a spring of water of the greatest purity, and unfailing in its flow even during the most protracted droughts'. Legend relates that a former higher outlet in a meadow was filled in by a certain Mr. Higgins, who was annoyed by villagers trespassing on his land to obtain water. Shortly after this unfriendly act, and while smoking his pipe one evening beside his fire, Higgins was suddenly startled by a rush of water at his feet. He presumed the spirit of the well had come to bear revenge, so he hurriedly re-opened the well at its present site to appease the ghost. The well has since then borne Higgin's name.

continued on page 52

49

Route 11

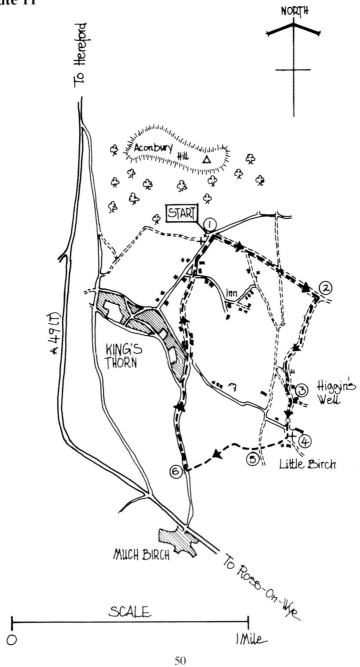

NORTH

To Hereford

Aconbury Hill

START
①
②

Inn

A 49 (T)

KING'S THORN

③ Higgin's Well

④

⑤ Little Birch

⑥

MUCH BIRCH

To Ross-On-Wye

SCALE

0   1 Mile

Route 11
Higgin's Well
3 miles

START *from Little Birch Methodist Chapel (OS Sheet 149 GR 506325) situated at the foot of Aconbury Hill mid-way between Ross-on-Wye and Hereford.*

ROUTE

1. *At the Methodist Chapel cross the road and follow a green lane for half a mile till passing Saddlebow Cottage on the right.*

2. *A few yards past this cottage turn sharp right along a tarmac lane gently descending to the Crow's Nest, a renovated house on the left. Continue ahead down a boggy track leading to Higgin's Well.*

3. *From the well take the right hand fork up a stony track to Little Birch church.*

4. *Beside the church follow a signed footpath leading past a bungalow. The path bears right through a field to a barn, where it goes alongside the left hand hedge to a gate leading on to a cart truck.*

5. *Cross the track and keep straight ahead along a muddy green lane to a field gate. Enter a field by the gate, turn left and descend to a footbridge crossing the Wriggle Brook. Continue ahead uphill keeping to the right hand hedge till reaching a gate between two cottages.*

6. *Turn right along a tarmac lane to Lower Wriggle Brook, where the right hand fork is followed to a minor crossroads. Proceed ahead along an unmade track gently ascending to a further crossroads, where the way ahead leads on to a road. Turn right and return to the chapel.*

ACCESS BY BUS
To King's Thorn from Hereford and Ross-on-Wye.

At Little Birch church see if you can locate the tomb of H. W. Southey J.P. who was mainly responsible for restoring Higgin's Well. The church is dedicated to St. Mary the Virgin and was rebuilt and enlarged in 1869 on the site of an earlier building. It is normally locked but its exterior and graveyard may be explored and examined.

The Wriggle Brook is a pretty meandering stream rising at Little Birch and flowing through unspoilt countryside to its junction with the river Wye at Hoarwithy. During the 18th and 19th centuries its swiftly flowing waters powered five working mills along its banks.

Refreshments Walkers are advised to bring their own and it is best not to drink the well water.

Castle Inn, Little Birch has limited refreshments and opening hours.

THE STEPS AT FOWNHOPE

52

Route 12

Paget's Wood: Brockhampton and Fownhope

Outline   Overdine ~ Paget's Wood ~ Common Hill ~ Nash Hill ~ River Wye ~ Capler Camp ~ Overdine.

Summary   This is another splendid ramble across the scenic hills of the Middle Wye Valley. Attractive field paths and lush green lanes lead to the Nature Reserve at Paget's Wood, where in a woodland glade a pair of crumbling lime kilns hide. Nash Hill offers astonishing panoramic views of the surrounding countryside with the silent grey spire of Fownhope church in the foreground. This thriving and spreading village can be visited for refreshments. Below the thickly wooded slopes of Capler Camp a quiet sinuous lane joins a delightful path following the banks of the silvery Wye, where nature has covered the old quays and quarries. After an energetic climb to the camp, the high double ramparts of the Iron Age fort can be examined. Hills, woods, village and riverside make this a lovely family walk with an easy to follow route using some stretches of the clearly waymarked Wye Valley Walk.

Attractions   The start and finish of this ramble follows the route of the Wye Valley Walk which is clearly waymarked with yellow arrows, and a map pack is available from Tourist Information Centres. This long distance path covers fifty attractive miles between the castle town of Chepstow and the cathedral city of Hereford. It closely follows the banks of the Wye and will soon be extended a further 25 miles on to Hay-on-Wye.

Before reaching Paget's Wood, a great oak tree presents an impressive and pleasing attraction. Its twisted and gnarled roots can be used as seats as one admires fine sweeping views of nearby hills and valleys. Glance up into its leafy branches and think of the wild life that it supports. Notice how it suffered some damage during its long life, many broken branches still lie beneath its shady canopy. The oak's fruit is the familiar acorn, a word derived from the Danish, meaning 'oak seed-grain' recalling its value as pig fodder.

Paget's Wood consists of sixteen acres of mixed woodland and is now owned by the Herefordshire Nature Trust. Yew, wild service, spindle and spurge-laurel thrust upward amongst ash, oak, birch, field maple, hazel and wild cherry. From early spring a wide variety of wild flowers will be seen and this peaceful setting attracts warblers, woodpeckers, goldcrests and treecreepers. Walk quietly and you may catch a glimpse of fallow deer, fox and stoat.

continued on page 56

Route 12

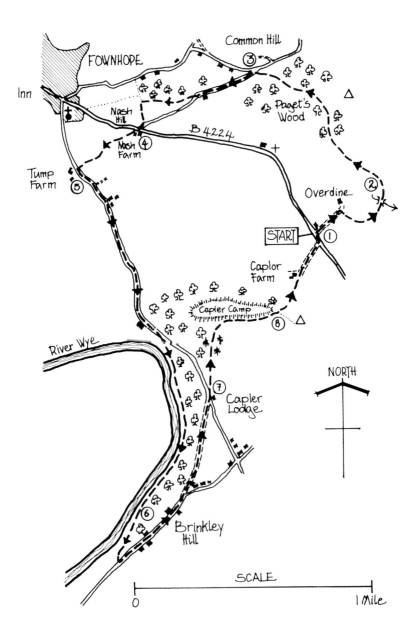

Route 12
Paget's Wood

6 miles

START *at the Wye Valley Walk sign (OS Sheet 149 GR 598335) leading to Overdine from the B4224 Fownhope to Ross road. Park on verge.*

ROUTE

1. *Follow the waymarks of the Wye Valley Walk along the track to Overdine then bear right through fields as directed by the yellow arrows. A brook is crossed where the path goes straight uphill to a stile. Here bear left to another stile beside a large oak.*

2. *Keep left through a small orchard and cross a stile leading on to a wide green lane which leads to a further stile into Paget's Wood. Follow the well defined woodland path as it veers to the right. This joins a bridleway which is followed to the left past partly concealed lime kilns, and out of the woods to a gate and stile. Keep to the right hand edge of this field to reach a tarmac lane at Common Hill.*

3. *Leave the route of the waymarked path and descend this lane. After passing a cottage on the left turn right to follow a signed footpath down a bank then sharp left over a makeshift stile leading into large meadows. Walk above the wooded slope and at Nash Hill go through a gap in the hedge leading into a narrow strip of grass. Here turn sharp left to reach a gate and a tarmac lane. Follow the lane to the right to meet the Fownhope road.*

4. *Cross the Fownhope road and continue ahead along a signed path through a gate leading to the right of Nash Farm. Keep close to the boundary wall then turn left over a stile. From here the right-of-way goes right through pastures with stiles in between until reaching steps descending to a tarmac lane opposite the entrance to Tump Farm. (To visit Fownhope's church, inn and shops, turn right).*

5. *Turn left along this lane for nearly a mile, passing isolated farms and cottages. Just beyond a stone cottage on the right bear right along a track signed 'Private Road' which leads down to the banks of the River Wye. Continue along the river bank for a mile.*

6. *By a clump of willow trees the path leaves the riverside by ascending a wooded slope. Upon reaching a tarmac lane at Brinkley Hill turn left and follow it for a quarter of a mile until reaching the old school. Here rejoin the waymarked route of the Wye Valley Walk proceeding left along a track behind the school building.*

Do not miss the lime kilns now almost hidden by undergrowth, simple earth mounds with stone archways below. During the 18th and 19th centuries limestone was conveyed from local pits and quarries along this track to be processed in these kilns. Alternate layers of limestone and fuel were placed in the hole at the top then fired from the furnace below. This method produced clinker which fell into the draw hole at the bottom, it was slated with water and crumbled into fine powder. The lime was used as mortar for building and as an agricultural fertiliser. In those days it was not uncommon to find tramps sleeping on top of kilns where a warm and comfortable night could be guaranteed. The best known lime-burner of all was John Clare (1793-1864) who wrote many poems about his rural existence. Another famous name associated with lime kilns was Turner (1775-1851) who featured them in many of his paintings.

From Nash Hill a descent is made into Fownhope, a village which is rapidly expanding around its ancient core. It is pleasantly situated between the Wye and the wooded slopes of Common Hill on the route of the old Hereford to Gloucester highway. The community have shops and inns, a school, village hall and an interesting church where a Norman tympanum and a 14th century parish chest provide unusual features. Outside stand 'Ye Olde Parish Stocks' re-erected by local churchmen in 1909 to preserve this relic of the past.

The last ascent of this walk is up Capler Camp standing at 600 feet, the site of an Iron Age hill fort. As a place of refuge this was ideal, natural steep slopes enclosed by double ramparts. The eastern entrance can be identified where foundations of a 17th century cottage was discovered during excavations. Far reaching views of the Black Mountains, Malvern Hills and May Hill are seen on a clear day from the top of this prehistoric site.

Refreshments   At the Green Man, Fownhope. Good selection of bar snacks. Garden with lovely views.

7. *Cross the road at Capler Lodge where the track continues through woods, and, as the arrows indicate, bear right through a young conifer plantation to a stile leading on to the ramparts of Capler Camp. Turn right where another stile leads on to the open part of the hill fort. Continue ahead between double ramparts and pass a stone building on the right.*

8. *Next be careful to bear left and descend a flight of wooden steps. Keep to a hedge on the left and continue to Capler Farm. Here turn left and immediately right, to follow a farm track back to the Fownhope road.*

ACCESS BY BUS   From Hereford to Fownhope.

Route 13

Broomy Hill: Breinton and Hereford

Outline   Breinton Spring ~ Hereford ~ Broomy Hill ~ Breinton Spring.

Summary   A combination of field paths, green lanes, suburban Hereford, and a lengthy stretch along the river Wye, make this an interesting and varied walk. At Broomy Hill the Herefordshire Waterworks Museum housed in a Victorian Pumping Station provides a halfway diversion for all the family. Despite uneven paths at the start, the remainder of the ramble follows level and well used routes which we found suitable to push a baby buggy, as long as there is no objection to lifting the vehicle over an assortment of stiles. Older children will enjoy the wide and shady green lanes, the attractive riverside, the Waterworks Museum and an unusual fresh water spring, while parents will be rewarded by liquid refreshments along the way.

Attractions   Broomy Hill lies on the western outskirts of Hereford where rows of large Victorian houses overlook the river Wye. The prominent landmark in this area is the tall tower of Broomy Hill Waterworks looming above the brick Pumping Station built in 1856. These fascinating waterworks have been converted into a museum where gleaming engines and brass pumps are operated by steam on certain days. Ring the Waterworks Museum (0432 274104) for times of opening and steam days.

Broomy Hill is reached by an easy route starting from Breinton, where a car park adjoins an intriguing oval mound believed to be the remains of a 12th century moated site which can be climbed upon and investigated. Below the earthwork, and beside the Wye, is a spring of pure water eternally gushing from sandstone rock. Cup your hands and taste this natural water, it is perfectly safe to drink. Nearby, and in sight is the parish church of Breinton, dedicated to St. Michael, which dates from the 12th century, but was mainly rebuilt in the 1860s.

The majority of Breinton's paths are kept in good order. They are waymarked with yellow arrows provided by the Country Landowner's Association, a welcome sight to walkers and riders. Green Lane is a delight, wide and wooded with narrow tree tunnels, a wayside pond, derelict farm buildings, open fields offering fine views of Credenhill, the Malvern Hills and Hereford city with the crooked spire of All Saints church clearly visible in the distance. Suddenly one arrives in Hereford

continued on page 60

Route 13

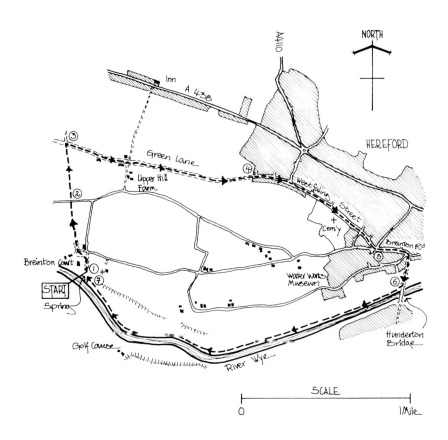

Route 13
Broomy Hill

5½ miles

START   *From Hereford follow the road to Breinton and park at the National Trust car park at Breinton Spring (OS Sheet 149 GR 472395).*

ROUTE

1. *Follow the track leading away from the banks of the river Wye, pass Breinton House, bear left through a swing gate, and walk across an orchard to another gate. Cross a lane and continue ahead along a driveway. Turn left through a field gate and then turn right to follow an undefined path alongside the right hand hedge. Proceed across two more fields to reach a road by the stile.*

2. *Cross the road and keep ahead along a well used path through fields till reaching a wide green lane.*

3. *Turn right along this lane. After passing a pond on your right and a derelict brick building on the left, bear slightly left to turn off the lane through a field gate. Continue in the same direction along a right-of-way which leads into Hereford. (If you wish to visit the Bay Horse Inn, turn left along a bridleway immediately after going through the field gate. You will see the Inn in the distance.)*

4. *At the outskirts of Hereford keep ahead, follow Westfaling Street across a roundabout and past a cemetery on your right to reach Breinton Road.*

5. *Proceed along Breinton Road and turn right into Broomy Hill. Immediately turn left down a slope to follow a cycle track going right to Hunderton Bridge.*

6. *Just before the bridge take a flight of steps on your right, which leads to the riverside. Here follow the clear path leading upstream through fields and over stiles past the Waterworks Museum and Belmont Golf course on the opposite bank. Continue along the river back to Breinton.*

7. *At Breinton keep left to visit the spring, then climb the steep path leading back to the car park.*

ACCESS BY BUS
   To Hereford from Hay-on-Wye, Ross-on-Wye, Gloucester, Monmouth and Ledbury.

where a quiet street leads past the town's cemetery before reaching Broomy Hill.

A cycle track shows how a new use can be made of a dismantled railway line and a redundant rail bridge. Great Western Way is a reminder of the days when trains of the Great Western Railway steamed along from Hereford across Hunderton bridge. This fine wrought iron bridge was erected in 1853; rebuilt and strengthened at the beginning of the century.

The return from Broomy Hill follows the banks of the river Wye for just over two miles. In midsummer the riverside is covered with Himalayan Balsam, an attractive sweet smelling pink flower which only became established in Herefordshire in the 1930s, but which spreads very rapidly along water courses and is now causing concern. Shake the seed pods and watch them explode and the seeds pop out. Amongst the Balsam grows tansy and yarrow. Lightweight canoes and home made rafts paddle past as fishermen try their luck along this sheltered stretch of the Wye.

Refreshments **The Bay Horse** is a small two bar Whitbread pub with a good line in cheap snacks. Decorated with brassy bits, it won't disappoint the famished walker.

The Antelope another Whitbread house, has a naval connection and suffered pangs of genuine remorse when its named ship suffered damage in the Falklands. (Snacks are available and children under supervision tolerated).

OLD HOUSE AT EATON BISHOP

Ruckall Common: Eaton Bishop

Outline   Eaton Bishop ~ Lower Eaton ~ Ruckall Common ~ Eaton Camp ~ Eaton Bishop.

Summary   Within sight of the tower and spire of Eaton Bishop church, this is a lush, green walk incorporating splendid, typically English parkland with sloping fields dotted with ancient oaks. The exceptionally good state of the Rights of Way makes this route easy to follow, although waving crops of wheat, barley, beans and peas will obstruct the field paths during early summer. A gentle downhill start leads to the banks of the river Wye. Here, dark and peaceful, the river flows lazily by, carrying the odd cheerful canoeist and families of mallards busily foraging with their offspring in the sedges. A wild and unspoilt stretch of riverbank is walked before ascending to Ruckall Common with its ancient camp site. Although a notable pub at Ruckall offers ample refreshments, a picnic under the shady arms of one of the centuries old oaks, using their fallen limbs as a table for your sandwiches and perhaps a wedge of fruit cake, takes some beating.

Attractions   Eaton Bishop church stands in a prominent position more than 300 feet above sea level. The lovely old building reveals traces of Saxon workmanship, a thick walled Norman tower and rare 14th century stained glass windows. In 1885 the Victorians undertook a major restoration costing £1,700.

   Shortly after leaving the church a sudden awareness of the 20th century intrudes, as the giant saucers of the Satellite Earth Station at Madley come into view. British Telecom, who operate this Tracking Centre, do not normally open to visitors.

   An impressive and continuous feature of this ramble is the excellent state of the footpaths, where signs, stiles and footbridges have been recently erected by a local voluntary group of active retirees. With the co-operation and help of the Hereford and Worcester County Council, Eaton Bishop Parish Council, and landowners, these improvements have taken place. They are to be congratulated and we hope that many more parishes will follow in their footsteps!

   In May, meadows of buttercups are fringed by hedges of creamy may. Soft shades of comfrey, tiny ground ivy, bright pink campion and strong smelling garlic grow prettily in the shade of ancient hawthorns.

continued on page 64

Route 14

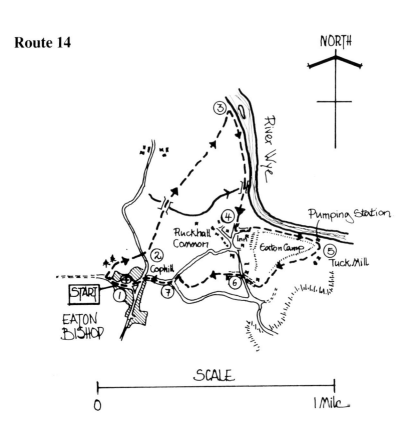

NORTH

River Wye

Pumping Station

③

④

Ruckhall Common

Inn

Eaton Camp

⑤

Tuck.Mill

②

Cophill

⑥

START

①

⑦

EATON BISHOP

SCALE

0   1 Mile

TREECREEPER

brown and white   13cm.

Route 14
Ruckall Common

3¼ miles

START *from Eaton Bishop church (OS Sheet 149 GR 443391). One mile from the Hereford to Hay-on-Wye road (B4349). Limited parking outside church or along lane.*

ROUTE

1. *Facing Eaton Bishop church turn left along a tarmac lane leading on to a track. Within 100 yards follow a footpath on the right, over a stile, and through a small fir coppice. Keep right of an open shed to reach a stile leading into a field. Walk straight across this to a road.*

2. *Cross the road, then follow a signed path which bears slightly left across a large field to arrive at a stile and footbridge lying to the left of a row of oaks. After crossing the bridge, keep ahead through fields where stiles clearly indicate the way. On approaching the river turn left over a stile on to a track which is followed to the banks of the Wye.*

3. *At the riverside turn right along an overgrown path and after crossing a footbridge bear diagonally right through a meadow. A stile leads on to a track which steeply ascends to meet a tarmac lane at Ruckall Common.*

4. *Follow the lane to the left, but before reaching the Ancient Camp Inn turn left along a signed footpath proceeding along the contours of Eaton Camp. A flight of steps descend to the banks of the river.*

5. *Keep right of the Pumping Station then turn sharp right along a track past Tuck Mill until a footpath sign directs the way going right over a stile. Bear right along an old overgrown track which veers right before reaching a road.*

6. *Continue across the road, go past Sunny Bank and enter a field where the right-of-way keeps to the right hand hedge. Cross a stile and turn left following a short track to another stile. In the next field keep to the left hand hedge heading for a stile leading into a larger field. From here walk straight through the crops or to avoid them turn right and walk around the field towards a stile to the right of a cottage at Cophill.*

7. *Cross the stile on to the road. Turn left, then bear right at the junction and follow the road over the crossroads, back to the church.*

ACCESS BY BUS
    To Eaton Bishop from Hereford.

The familiar call of cuckoos kept us company throughout the walk and the old rhyme comes to mind:

The cuckoo comes in April
Changes his tune in middle of June
In July he flies away.
How many other such verses can be recalled?

At Ruckall Common a well-defined riverside path skirts the defences of Eaton Camp. This is a promontory Iron Age hillfort on a high bluff between the river Wye and the Cage Brook. The Tuck Mill beside the brook was in existence in 1750 but a modern building now stands on the stone footings of the mill. Water-powered tuck mills were involved in cloth manufacture but this one was also used as a corn mill in the 1880s.

Refreshments At the Ancient Camp Inn. Better than average fare available at this attractively sited pub overlooking the river Wye. Children and walkers welcome.

ARTHUR'S STONE

Arthur's Stone: Dorstone

Outline Dorstone ~ Spoon Lane ~ Arthur's Stone ~ Crossway ~ Dorstone.

Summary This part of the Wye Valley in West Herefordshire is significantly less developed and inhabited. As is often the case in such quiet untouched places every right-of-way vanishes from lack of former usage as a path to church, work or school. It makes a challenging and attractive proposition for all members of the family to tackle and explore. From Dorstone a level start leads across fields and green lanes where superb views abound as one climbs higher towards the ridge of green hills rising over 900 feet above the village snugly nestling below, beside the banks of the tiny river Dore.

With baby on our backs we progressed through beautiful Welsh Border farming country to attain our goal, then sat and contemplated the serene and extensive view from Arthur's Stone, a famous prehistoric chambered tomb high above the village.

While not ideal for the infirm, this walk can be hugely enjoyed by adults and even determined toddlers, who will feel amply compensated for their expended energies by the sight of Arthur's memorial and the panoramic scenes of tranquil meadow, wood and stream all around.

Attractions Dorstone is an attractive village in the Golden Valley, near the market town of Hay-on-Wye. Pretty cottages, an inn, shop and post office encircle a neat green where a water fountain and seat make a pleasant and useful feature. St. Faith's church not far from the village centre was founded in 1256 but mostly rebuilt in 1889. Nearby stands a wooden mound, all that remains of a Norman motte and bailey castle. The tiny river Dore gave the valley its name in Norman times when they translated the Welsh word for water 'dwr' to 'd'or', gold in French.

Later as the disused railway track is crossed it is easy to imagine steam trains thundering between Hay and Pontrilas. The Golden Valley Railway operated between 1881 and 1957; a station once stood on the outskirts of Dorstone village.

The interestingly named Spoon Lane is a typical example of an ancient byway, no longer needed, it lies forgotten and neglected. If it is ever cleared it will provide a wonderfully peaceful route for walkers and riders. Holly, hawthorn, hazel, oak and elder enclose the lane and views of this beautiful undulating countryside can be fully appreciated. After a

continued on page 68

65

Route 15

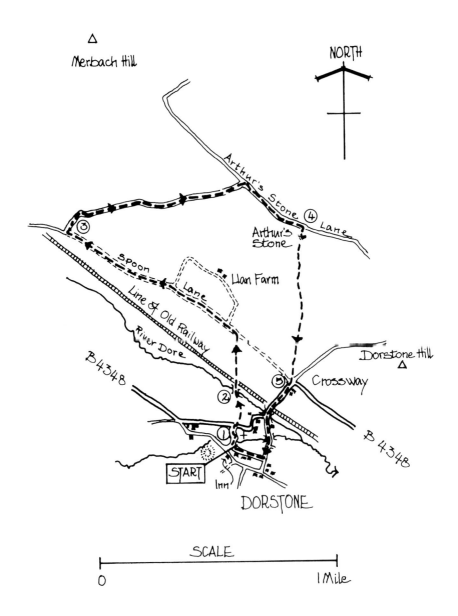

Route 15

Arthur's Stone

4 miles

START *from Dorstone village green, (OS Sheet 148 or 161 GR 314416) a turning off the B4348 leading to Hay-on-Wye.*

ROUTE

1. *At Dorstone village green follow a lane signed 'to the church', and continue along a tarmac footpath leading to the left of the churchyard. Cross a road and enter Dorstone Playing Fields by a swing gate. Follow an undefined path straight ahead to a stile in the fence. Here proceed across the field and cross the river Dore by a footbridge. A stile here leads on to a disused railway track.*

2. *Walk over the old railway line, climb a wire fence, (missing stile reported), then proceed across a field to its left hand corner where an overgrown stile leads into Spoon Lane. Turn left along this sunken green lane, but if overgrowth obstructs the way, continue through fields alongside until the way ahead is clear, and can be followed to its junction with a tarmac lane.*

3. *Turn right along this tarmac lane which twists and turns as it steeply ascends the ridge. At a 'T' junction turn right to Arthur's Stone.*

4. *From this prehistoric site follow a signed path on the right which descends across the middle of two meadows, then through a succession of field gates keeping the hedges on your right, until half way down when the hedge should be on the left (after taking the right hand gate beside a small elder tree). Proceed till reaching the road at Crossway.*

5. *Follow this road to the right, take the first turning on the left, then turn right to follow the road back to Dorstone village green.*

ACCESS BY BUS

To Dorstone from Hay-on-Wye and Hereford.

quiet picnic here in the autumn sun we finished our meal with a handful of juicy blackberries foraged from bountiful brambles.

A scenic ridge runs between Dorstone and Merbach Hills rising to over 900 feet affording tremendous views across the Wye Valley. Arthur's Stone Lane leads along the ridge to a prehistoric site now in the care of English Heritage. King Arthur, however, has no connection whatever with this ancient edifice which was constructed long before his time. It is, in fact, a burial tomb built between 2000 and 3000 B.C., consisting of a chamber and entrance passage once under a mound of earth which has been either washed away or removed. Huge stones enclose the chamber, supporting a broken capstone measuring nineteen by eleven feet. The entrance tunnel is enclosed by massive stones and is also uncovered. Climb on to the stones and explore the tunnel, remembering this was a family or community burial vault of many years ago. Neolithic and Bronze Age flints have been discovered in the surrounding area.

The return to Dorstone is a pleasant downhill ramble across soft sheep-filled pastures. Between Crossway and the village watch out for an iron milepost on the edge of the road stating that from Dorstone Parish Hay-on-Wye is six miles and Peterchurch three. This marker was erected in the mid 1800s by the local Turnpike Trust for those travelling by horseback or in horse drawn vehicles along the toll road from Hay to Ross-on-Wye.

Refreshments   The Pandy Inn at Dorstone provides snacks in bar or garden.

HAY CASTLE

Route 16   3 miles
The Warren: Hay-on-Wye

Outline   Hay-on-Wye ~ Bailey Walk ~ The Warren ~ Hay-on-Wye.

Summary   From a scenic car park below the slopes of the Black Mountains this short ramble follows field and riverside paths around the pleasantly situated Welsh town of Hay-on-Wye. From Hay bridge the well used Bailey Walk leads to the Warren, a beautiful open space offering plenty of opportunities for the young to explore, hills of tall bracken, wooded mounds, banks of wild pink and white flowers, acres of grassland and delightful picnic sites. After this wild and natural place a more sombre route passes Hay church, twisting and turning between houses and cottages, crossing small bridges over shallow streams before reaching the town. Time must be allowed to explore the largely unspoilt buildings of Hay where the charred remains of a Norman castle dominates this place now famous for its secondhand bookshops.

Attractions   Hay-on-Wye is a pleasant Welsh border market town nestling between the banks of the Wye and the eastern ridge of the Black Mountains. The ruins of Hay castle cannot be missed with its ill-fated history dating back to the 1200s. Built by a Norman Marcher Lord it suffered fire damage in 1231 and after many centuries of intrigue and changes of ownership the castle was burnt down again in 1939 and 1977. Other notable buildings found in the town's narrow twisting streets are the Butter Market of 1833 and a clock tower erected in 1884. Secondhand bookshops abound, offering a vast range of subjects to visitors of all ages who make their pilgrimage to Hay in search of enlightenment.

A quiet rural path around the outskirts of the town leads to the site of an ancient ford crossing the river Wye, used before the building of Hay's first bridge in 1763. Floods and frosts have played havoc with a succession of bridges until the erection of the present ugly but sturdy structure in 1958 by the County Council.

In 1884 Sir Joseph Bailey, Lord of the Manor, laid out a delightful riverside walk, thereby preserving a centuries old right-of-way leading from the bridge to St. Mary's church. The Bailey Walk extends to the Warren, a wild and over-grown beauty spot where picnics can be enjoyed above the swift waters of the Wye. Children can stand beside the tall pink flowered Himalayan Balsam and guess the height of this sickly sweet smelling flower, then make tunnels through thick ferns and follow narrow paths up steep wooded banks.

continued on page 72

Route 16

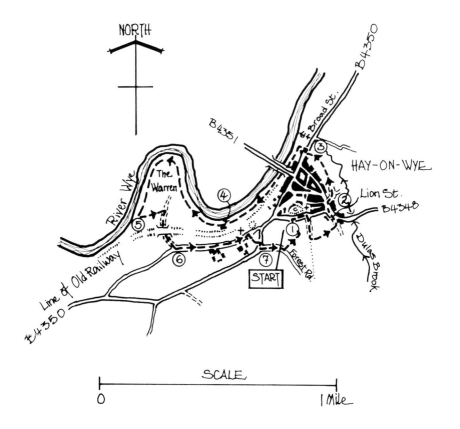

NORTH

B4350

B4351

4 Broad St.

HAY-ON-WYE

River Wye

The Warren

Lion St.

B4348

③

④

②

①

⑤

Dulas Brook

Line of Old Railway

B4350

⑥

⑦

Forest Rd.

START

SCALE

0   1 Mile

Route 16
The Warren
3 miles

START *The car park (OS Sheet 148 or 161 GR 228423) beside the Tourist Information Centre at Hay-on-Wye.*

ROUTE

1. *From the car park turn right along the road and within 200 yards follow an Offa's Dyke Path sign to the right down a short track. Enter a field by a swing gate. Go straight on for about 150 yards, then turn left over a stile. Cross a paddock to a further stile leading on to a lane. Bear left on to the road and turn left along Lion Street.*

2. *Just before the Black Lion Inn bear right down a narrow lane, and take the left hand fork leading to a stile. A rough grass path follows along the left hand hedge of a sloping field to a stile in the left hand corner.*

3. *Cross Broad Street, turn right and beyond the veterinary surgery turn left along a track leading to the river Wye. Follow the river bank to the left under Hay Bridge and continue beside the Wye following the Bailey Walk.*

4. *On passing Warren Cottage a gate leads into the Warren. Here bear right along the riverside leading around a horseshoe bend and up a wooded slope.*

5. *Upon meeting a stone wall cross the stile leading into a meadow, where the right-of-way continues close to the riverbank for a further 100 yards. At this point turn left across the meadow to a stile leading on to a track and follow it to the right under the disused railway bridge to the road.*

6. *Turn left and just past St. Mary's church turn right through a swing gate, where a winding path crosses and re-crosses a narrow brook.*

7. *At the road turn right, then left along Forest Road till reaching a footpath on the left (before a house called Camelot). Follow this path through fields and back to the car park.*

ACCESS BY BUS

To Hay-on-Wye from Hereford.

From the Warren a bridleway leads under an arch of the disused Hereford, Hay, Brecon Railway. Opened in 1864 it replaced a former horsedrawn tramway constructed in the 18th century to carry coal from the Abergavenny and Brecon Canal. The church of St. Mary's is worth a visit before taking a pretty town path alongside the Login Brook. Swan Well is passed, now a trickling spring which in earlier times was said to cure sprains of hands and feet. The car park is soon reached with expansive views of the surrounding countryside and the Tourist Information Centre adjacent offers detailed guides of the town and other useful literature.

Refreshments   The Granary, Hay-on-Wye. Selection of wholefoods in pleasant surroundings.

Plenty of other tea rooms and pubs to choose from.

RIVER AT DORSTONE

72

Appendices

ROUTES IN ORDER OF DIFFICULTY

Starting with the easiest:

Route   4 - *Forest Ponds — 2½ miles*
Route   5 - *Yat Ferry — 4 miles*
Route 14 - *Ruckall Common — 3¼ miles*
Route   6 - *Luke Brook — 2 miles*
Route   9 - *Sellack Boat — 4½ miles*
Route 13 - *Broomy Hill — 5½ miles*
Route 16 - *The Warren — 3 miles*
Route 10 - *Ruined Church — 2 miles*
Route 11 - *Higgin's Well — 3 miles*
Route   8 - *Rudhall Brook — 6½ miles*
Route 12 - *Paget's Wood — 6 miles*
Route   1 - *365 Steps — 3 miles*
Route   3 - *Naval Temple — 3½ miles*
Route   7 - *Chase Hillfort — 3¼ miles*
Route   2 - *Penterry Church — 4½ miles*
Route 15 - *Arthur's Stone — 4 miles*

PUBLIC TRANSPORT IN THE WYE VALLEY

The area covered by this book is not particularly well served by public transport, but small new companies appear from time to time.
The only railway stations are in Hereford and Chepstow.
Bus companies run an infrequent service; timetables need to be carefully consulted.

British Rail .... Tel. Hereford 266534
Lugg Valley Motors .... Tel. Leominster 2759
National Welsh Omnibus Services .... Tel. Cardiff 371331
Red and White Buses .... Tel. Chepstow 3565
Smith's Motors .... Tel. Ledbury 2953
Yeoman's Canyon Travel .... Tel. Hereford 56201

TOURIST INFORMATION CENTRES IN THE WYE VALLEY

Chepstow, The Gatehouse, 02912-3772.
Tintern, Tintern Abbey, 02918-431.
Monmouth, 5 Church Street, 0600-3899.
Coleford, 24 Market Place, 0594-36307.
Ross-on-Wye, 20 Broad Street, 0989-62768.
Hereford, Town Hall, 0432-268430.
Hay-on-Wye, The Car Park, 0497-820144.

73

WET WEATHER ALTERNATIVES IN THE WYE VALLEY completely or partly under cover.

It is advisable to check times of opening before a visit is made.

MUSEUMS AND CRAFT WORKSHOPS

The Shambles, Church Street, Newent; a museum of Victorian life of 100 years ago. Open: Easter to October. Refreshments.

Chepstow Museum, Bridge Street, Chepstow 5981; local history collections showing Chepstow's industries of the past. Open: March to October.

Monmouth Museum, Priory Street, Monmouth 3519; a unique collection of Nelson's life with local history centre. Open: all year.

Mortimers Cross Mill, Lucton; an 18th century watermill on the river Lugg. Open: April to September on Thursdays.

Broomy Hill Engines, Waterworks Museum, Hereford 274104; 19th century water pumping station with occasional working steam engines. Open: August and Sundays in June and July. In steam Bank Holidays.

Rural Heritage Museum, Doward, Symonds Yat 890474; permanent display of a large collection of historic farm machinery. Open: Easter to October, picnic site.

Dean Heritage Centre, Soudley, Cinderford, Dean 22170; an award winning project featuring the life and history of the Forest of Dean. Open: all year, refreshments, picnic site.

Folk Museum, Wolvesnewton, Chepstow, 02915-231; unusual 18th century farm buildings with Victorian exhibitions. Open: April to September. Refreshments. Picnic site.

Cowdy Glass Workshop, Culver Street, Newent, 0531-821173; glassblowing by skilled craftsmen. Open: all year.

Churchill Gardens Museum, Venns Lane, Hereford 267409; furniture, paintings and costumes. Open: on certain days throughout year.

Hereford City Museum, Broad Street, Hereford 268121; exhibitions, natural history, archaeology, local history, art gallery. Open: all year.

Museum of Cider, Whitecross Road, Hereford 54307; displays of traditional farm cider making. Open: April to October.

The Old House, High Town, Hereford 268121; a Jacobean house furnished in 17th century style. Open: all year.

St. John Medieval Museum, Conningsby Hospital, Widemarsh Street, Hereford 272837; museum and chapel in buildings dating back to 13th century. Open Easter to September.

Ross-on-Wye Candlemakers, Old Gloucester Road, Ross 63697; workshop manufacturing all types of candles. Open: Monday to Friday.

CASTLES, HOUSES AND CHURCHES

Penhow Castle, near Newport, 0633-400800; a tour around a lived-in Welsh castle complete with Soundalive Walkman. Open: Easter to September. Refreshments.

Eastnor Castle, Ledbury 2305; a mock gothic castle of 1812 with impressive interior and armoury. Open: Sundays, Easter to September. Refreshments. Picnic site.

Burton Court, Erdisland, Pembridge 231; the house has a 14th century great hall with displays of costumes and working models. Open: May to September. Refreshments.

Dinmore Manor, Hereford 71322; unusual cloisters and music room. 12th century chapel. Open: all year.

Pembridge Castle, Welsh Newton, 060084-226; a small 13th century fortified castle. Open: Thursdays, May to September.

Moccas Court, Moccas, 09817-381; 18th century house designed by Adam on the banks of the river Wye. Open: April to October on Thursdays.

Sufton Court, Mordiford, 043273-268; Palladian mansion by James Wyatt. Open: August and September.

Hellen's, Much Marcle, 053184-668; interesting house dating back to 13th century. Open: Easter to September.

The Old Grammar School, Ledbury; restored timber framed building in cobbled church street. Open: May to September.

Kempley church; medieval wall paintings.

Newland church; 'Cathedral of the Forest' with Miner's brass.

Pauntley church; associated with Dick Whittington.

Bredwardine church; where Francis Kilvert, Victorian diarist, was curate.

Brockhampton church; built in the style of the Arts and Crafts movement.

Eaton Bishop church; fine medieval windows.

Fownhope church; Norman tympanum and 14th century wooden chest.

Garway church; founded by Knights Templars.

Goodrich church; burial place of Thomas Swift, grandfather of Dean Swift, author of Gulliver's Travels.

Hoarwithy church; unique Italian design of 1880s.

Holme Lacy church; with impressive memorials of the Scudamore family.

Kilpeck church; Norman with unusual carvings.

Mordiford church; with legend featuring a green dragon.

Ross-on-Wye church; 13th century with monuments of Rudhall family.

Welsh Newton church; where John Kemble, Catholic martyr, is buried.

Dixton church; Early English period situated on the banks of the Wye.

Much Marcle church; a family seat under an ancient yew tree in the graveyard.

Hereford Cathedral; chained library and crypt with Diocesan treasures.

SPORTING FACILITIES under cover.

Ross-on-Wye Swimming Pool, Ross-on-Wye 62883.

Five Acres Campus Leisure Centre, Dean 35388.

Wyedean Sports Centre, Chepstow 5347.

West Mercia Equestrian Centre, Yarkhill. Tarrington 255.

Hereford Swimming Baths, Hereford 272512.

Hereford Leisure Centre, Hereford 271959.

Monmouth Leisure Centre, Monmouth 2646.

Chepstow Leisure Centre, Chepstow 3832.

TRAINS, CAVES AND WILDLIFE ATTRACTIONS Indoors.

Clearwell Caves, Coleford, 0594 23700; a tour of ancient iron mines in the Forest of Dean. Open: March to October. Refreshments. Picnic site.

Tintern Station, Tintern, 02918-566; reconstructed railway station, signal box with display of the Wye Valley Railway. Open: Easter to October. Refreshments. Picnic site.

Bulmer Railway Centre, Hereford 834430; steam locomotive and other rolling stock. Some steam events. Open: April to September, (weekends).

Newent Butterfly Centre, Birches Lane, Newent, 0531-821800; tropical butterflies and natural history exhibition. Open: Easter to October. Refreshments.

Falconry Centre, Newent, 0531-820286; comprehensive display of birds of prey. Open: February to November. Refreshments. Picnic site.

"World of Butterflies", Whitchurch, Symonds Yat 0600-890655; butterflies in a tropical atmosphere flying freely. Open: Easter to October.

Dean Forest Railway, Norchard Steam Centre, Lydney, 0594 43423; railway engines, coaches and wagons. Static display with steam days. Open: daily. Steam days on Bank Holidays.

G.W.R. Railway Museum, Coleford, 0594-33569; goods shed, steam locos, signal box, photographs and models. Open: daily except Mondays. Refreshments.

BIBLIOGRAPHY

Charles Heath, Excursions Down the Wye, 1826.
Wye Valley Map Pack, 1980-83.
Wyndcliff Nature Trail, Gwent Nature Trust.
Ivor Waters, Turnpike Roads, 1985.
Chris Barber, Exploring Gwent, 1984.
Herefordshire Directories, 1858, 1867 & 1902.
S. D. Coates & D. G. Tucker, Water Mills of the Middle Wye, 1983.
Rev. Bannister, Place Names of Herefordshire, 1916.
N. Pevsner, Buildings of Herefordshire, 1963.
AA/OS Leisure Guide to the Wye Valley, 1988.
Bob Cross, Industrial Wyedean, 1982.
Forestry Commission, Boy's Grave and Cannop Trail, 1974.
St. Michaels Church, Eaton Bishop.
Trans. of Woolhope Club, Vol. XLV 1985 pt. 1.
Arthur Mee, Herefordshire, 1948.
H. & J. Hurley, Ross-on-Wye Walkabout, 1986.
H. Edlim, Tree Key, 1978.
Herefordshire & Worcestershire County Council, Herefordshire Countryside Treasures, 1981.
H. Hurley, Wyedean Walks, 1983.
National Trust, The Kymin.
H. & J. Hurley, Rambles & Refreshments, 1988.
Hay-on-Wye Guide
G. Fairs, A History of the Hay, 1972.
Forestry Commission, Tintern Forest.
R. Howell, Fedw Villages, 1985.
Oxford Literary Guide, 1977.
Sir W. Addison, Old Roads of England, 1980.
Hereford & Radnor Nature Trust, Guide to Reserves
K. Kissack, River Wye, 1978.
H. & J. Hurley, Paths & Pubs of the Wye Valley, 1986.

PENTERRY CHURCH

PICNIC SITE AT CANNOP PONDS

FAMILY WALKS SERIES

Family Walks in the North Yorkshire Dales. Howard Beck. ISBN 0 907758 52 5.

Family Walks in West Yorkshire. Howard Beck. ISBN 0 907758 43 6.

Family Walks in Three Peaks and Malham. Howard Beck. ISBN 0 907758 42 8.

Family Walks in South Yorkshire. Norman Taylor. ISBN 0 907758 25 8.

Family Walks in the North Wales Borderlands. Gordon Emery. ISBN 0 907758 50 9.

Family Walks in Cheshire. Chris Buckland. ISBN 0 907758 29 0.

Family Walks in the Staffordshire Peak and Potteries. Les Lumsdon. ISBN 0 907758 34 7.

Family Walks in the White Peak. Norman Taylor. ISBN 0 907758 09 6.

Family Walks in the Dark Peak. Norman Taylor. ISBN 0 907758 16 9.

Family Walks in Snowdonia. Laurence Main. ISBN 0 907758 32 0.

Family Walks in Mid Wales. Laurence Main. ISBN 0 907758 27 4.

Family Walks in South Shropshire. Marian Newton. ISBN 0 907758 30 4.

Family Walks in the Teme Valley. Camilla Harrison. ISBN 0 907758 45 2.

Family Walks in Hereford and Worcester. Gordon Ottewell. ISBN 0 907758 20 7.

Family Walks around Cardiff and the Valleys. Gordon Hindess. ISBN 0 907758 54 1.

Family Walks in the Wye Valley. Heather and Jon Hurley. ISBN 0 907758 26 6.

Family Walks in Warwickshire. Geoff Allen. ISBN 0 907758 53 3.

Family Walks around Stratford and Banbury. Gordon Ottewell. ISBN 0 907758 49 5.

Family Walks in the Cotswolds. Gordon Ottewell. ISBN 0 907758 15 0.

Family Walks in South Gloucestershire. Gordon Ottewell. ISBN 0 907758 33 9.

Family Walks in Oxfordshire. Laurence Main. ISBN 0 907758 38 X

Family Walks around Bristol, Bath and the Mendips. Nigel Vile. ISBN 0 907758 19 3.

Family Walks in Wiltshire. Nigel Vile. ISBN 0 907758 21 5.

Family Walks in Berkshire and North Hampshire. Kathy Sharp. ISBN 0 907758 37 1.

Family Walks on Exmoor and the Quantocks John Caswell. ISBN 0 907758 46 0.

Family Walks in Mendip, Avalon and Sedgemoor. Nigel Vile. ISBN 0 907758 41 X.

Family Walks in Cornwall. John Caswell. ISBN 0 907758 55 X.

Family Walks on the Isle of Wight. Laurence Main. ISBN 0 907758 56 8.

Family Walks in North West Kent. Clive Cutter. ISBN 0 907758 36 3.

Family Walks in the Weald of Kent and Sussex. Clive and Sally Cutter. ISBN 0 907758 51 7.

_____

The Publishers, D. J. Mitchell and E. G. Power welcome suggestions for further titles in this Series; and will be pleased to consider manuscripts relating to Derbyshire from new or established authors.
_____